The Model in Practice 2

Using the EFQM Excellence Model to deliver continuous improvement

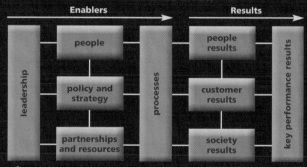

The Excellence Model

© 1999 EFQM

British Quality
FOUNDATION

Acknowledgements

> "If I have been able to see further than others, it is because I have stood on the shoulders of giants."
>
> Sir Isaac Newton

There has been such positive feedback on *The Model in Practice*, originally published in 2000, that we had little problem in answering the question of whether or not we should develop a sequel.

The Model in Practice has been an outstanding success for the BQF, being seen as our most satisfying product or service in our 2002 Customer Satisfaction survey.

We have had requests for more examples of good practice, and calls for further understanding of the linkages inherent in the model. Coupled with the growing appreciation of the potential value in the Fundamental Concepts of Excellence, there is an overwhelming case for the publication of *The Model in Practice 2*, which addresses each of these issues.

We are indebted to the many organisations who have shared their material so willingly and openly with us, in our pursuit of the 96 fresh vignettes that we have been privileged to select. There is a cumulative list of organisations contributing case study material in Appendix A1.

The European Centre for Business Excellence has again carried out the research for us, and to them, the contributors and all those who have been interviewed during the compilation of the book, we are very grateful.

Special recognition is due to those who have driven the development and co-ordination of this book over the past twelve months, and these include: Kay Aitken, Joachim Bauer, Lorraine Guyot, Ray Louden, Steve Tanner and Natalie Wheelan.

Once again though, as with so much of the work of the BQF, an essential ingredient has been the inspiration and support of our networking groups and members to whom we are as grateful as ever.

John Smith
July 2002

The British Quality Foundation exists to help organisations of all kinds to improve their performance. We are an independent, not for profit, membership organisation and we have a wide range of services, most of which are available to both members and non-members.

The services include:

- seminars on best practice and performance improvement;*
- networking groups for sharing and learning from best practice;*
- information and advice;*
- web services such as discussion groups;*
- membership magazine;*
- training;*
- benchmarking projects;
- research;
- study tour to the USA and other countries;
- wide range of publications;
- annual business excellence awards;
- help and advice on using the Excellence Model, Europe's leading performance improvement methodology;
- special services for small firms, the public sector and the voluntary sector.

*These services are only available to members.

T + 44 (0) 20 7654 5000
F + 44 (0) 20 7654 5001
E mail@quality-foundation.co.uk
W www.quality-foundation.co.uk

British Quality FOUNDATION

European Centre for Business Excellence

T + 44 (0) 113 244 9434
F + 44 (0) 113 234 1988
E contactus@ecforbe.com
W www.ecforbe.com

European Centre *for* Business Excellence

Contents

Chapter 1 Introduction

1.1 | About this Book

*T*he Model in Practice 2 builds on the research and methodology used in the *The Model in Practice*. You need no previous experience of business excellence to understand and use either book for the benefit of your organisation.

Examples of how different organisations are using the Model are an important feature of both books. Those provided here continue to emphasise the achievements of organisations in all sectors and add to the growing bank of best practice examples available. Reading these will inspire you to adopt and apply the Model within your own organisation.

The Model in Practice 2 has also been designed to help you address specific performance improvement issues through Links to the Fundamental Concepts. These offer an important interface with the business planning process. Do you want to work on improved motivation in your employees, or more efficient management practice? This book could help you to establish, prioritise and take action on improvement activities. Furthermore, we have used its methodology in our new software programme, *BQFsnapshot*, to develop what we consider to be 64 of the most important issues in today's working environment.

All the data and examples in this book are from UK-based organisations (see Appendix A1) and have been selected on the basis of being practical

examples of the Excellence Model in use. The British Quality Foundation (BQF) acknowledges all contributors – these include award-winners and other exemplar organisations – and thanks them for sharing their practice.

1.2 | The Fundamental Concepts of Excellence

Truly excellent organisations are measured by their ability to achieve and sustain outstanding results for all their stakeholders, such as customers, employees, shareholders and the community. This requires a management approach based on eight fundamental concepts:

Results Orientation: The needs of stakeholders are met and balanced. Stakeholders may include employees, customers, suppliers, shareholders and society.

Customer Focus: There is a clear understanding of the needs of both current and potential customers, and a passion for meeting needs and exceeding expectations.

Leadership and Constancy of Purpose: Leaders have a clear sense of direction and purpose, which they communicate effectively throughout the organisation.

Management by Process and Facts: All activities are managed in a systematic and effective way, taking into account all stakeholders' perceptions.

People Development and Involvement: A culture of trust and empowerment that allows all employees to develop and contribute to their full potential.

Continuous Learning, Improvement and Innovation: Knowledge is shared to maximise performance, with learning, innovation and improvement encouraged.

Partnership Development: There are mutually beneficial relationships with all partners.

Public Responsibility: The organisation fosters a positive and mutually beneficial relationship with society and the community.

N.B. There is no significance in the order of these concepts.

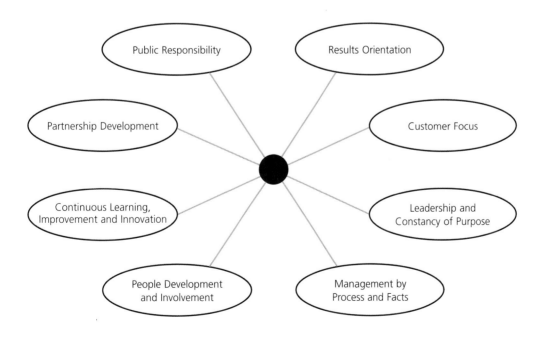

Driving Business Improvement Using the Model

The fundamental concepts behind the Model have been described previously, but the key question is 'How does the Model help drive business improvement?'

This is achieved through the application of RADAR philosophy, which is at the heart of the Model. It consists of four elements:

The philosophy is that an organisation needs to:

- *Determine the **Results** it is aiming for from its policy and strategy*
- *Plan and develop an integrated set of **Approaches***
- ***Deploy** the approaches, then*
- ***Assess** and **Review** these approaches, to identify, prioritise, plan and implement improvements.*

The Excellence Model has nine criteria that are broken down into two main groups, enablers and results. The five enablers are the things an organisation does in order to achieve the desired results. This result/enabler breakdown provides a valuable way for you to classify your organisation's activities and performance.

The theme of innovation and learning spans the Model and reinforces the feedback mechanisms that drive the improvement in your organisation's performance.

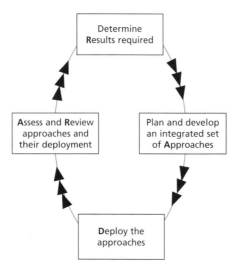

The Excellence Model

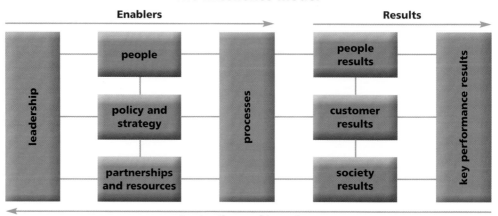

© 1999 EFQM. The Model is a registered trademark of EFQM

This book is structured around the nine criteria of the Model, and demonstrates the linkages between each of them, e.g. the ways in which the 'People' approaches drive the 'People' results.

1.4 | Benefits from Practising Excellence in Business

Business Excellence is not just another initiative, but a way of pulling several initiatives together in a focused and practical way. There is wide-ranging evidence from around the world that supports the benefits to be gained from following a philosophy of Excellence in business. This data comes from research into organisations that have won national and international Excellence awards, such as the UK Quality Award, the European Quality Award, the Japanese Deming Prize and the Malcolm Baldrige National Quality Award (MBNQA) in the USA, studies of Quality Award winning organisations proving that TQM improves the operating performance of an organisation.

It includes:

• Research, carried out by the European Centre for Business Excellence supported by the BQF and published in the 'X-Factor' report, reveals overwhelming verification of the links between Excellence, improved business performance and outstanding business results.

• A study of European companies using the concepts of Excellence showed that these companies out-performed their industry median, on four different financial indicators over a five-year period. For example, profit per employee in 79% of the companies was higher, 76% of the companies had a higher return on assets and 76% of the companies showed higher profit margins than their industry medians.

• The US National Institute of Standards and Technology hypothetically invested in $1000 of stock in each of the publicly traded American Baldrige Award winners over a seven-year period. These stocks outperformed the Standard and Poor's 500 (equivalent to the FTSE 100) index by between 3 and 3.5 to 1.

• A study of the Japanese Deming Prize-winners between 1961 and 1980 concluded that most companies had an upward trend in all key performance indicators and maintained this performance above the industry average.

• A study carried out over 5 years into the effects of TQM after the first year of implementation. Results showed that winners of various quality awards (from international to smaller scale awards) outperformed their benchmark in many different aspects of their performance. The study also measured the improved stock prices of almost all of the 140 award winners.

(refer to Appendix 2 for references).

1.5 | Chapter 3 Layout

Chapter 3 of this book is divided into sections according to the nine criteria of the Model, and each section is introduced by the definition of that criterion and its sub-criteria, plus an illustration of linkages between the sub-criteria within that criterion, and between all the enabler criteria.

Each of the nine sections then examines the sub-criteria that combine to make up the criterion, with each sub-criterion occupying a double-page spread, containing the definitions of the criterion and sub-criterion, plus a list of activities within an organisation that the particular sub-criterion could be applied to.

For each sub-criterion there are three examples to illustrate how it is put into practice in three different types of organisation – a large private sector company, a large public sector organisation and a small-to-medium business, or a division of a large private sector organisation. The logo at the top of the box cross-references to that in Appendix 1 to indicate which of these three sectors the example is from.

The lower boxes for each sub-criterion indicate the links to the fundamental concepts. Further links can be investigated within *BQFsnapshot*.

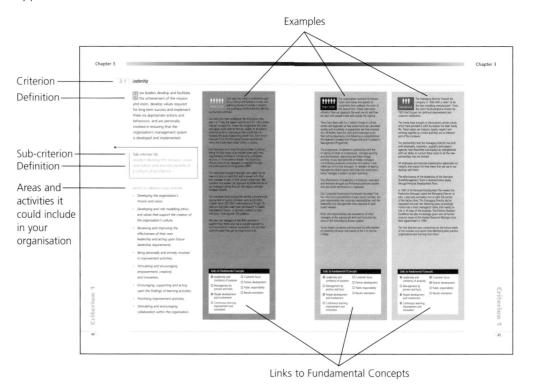

Examples

Criterion

Definition

Sub-criterion
Definition

Areas and
activities it
could include
in your
organisation

Links to Fundamental Concepts

2.1 | Introduction

As in version 1, this chapter shows how the examples in this book, together with other sources of information, can help you implement improvement in your organisation. Space does not allow a comprehensive description of all improvement approaches, but there is enough detail in this chapter to get you started.

It begins by describing a simple change process that you may use. This has four key steps, based around the RADAR (Results, Approach, Deployment, Assessment and Review) approach that underpins the philosophy of Excellence, described in Chapter 1.

A key feature of the approach is that it focuses on the results that you want to achieve. It makes use of the linkages within the Model and refers to the examples in Chapter 3 as a source of ideas for improvement action. The examples provided in the previous version can also be used in the same way.

In addition to referring to the examples, this chapter also includes other approaches that you may wish to consider, including some widely used and well-recognised tools and techniques. This should further assist you in the implementation of improvements, as the examples provide ideas and aid communication of the benefits of using the Excellence Model. These have been revised and updated with current approaches in addition to those provided in Version 1.

2.2 | A Simple Change Process Using RADAR

2.2.1 Introduction

RADAR, described in Chapter 1, is based on the widely known 'Plan-Do-Check-Act' continuous improvement cycle that some organisations have been following since the 1950s.

The concept is to:

Plan what you need to do to achieve your goals.

Do the action/activity.

Check or review that the action/activity was successful.

Act on the results of the review, for example, by taking additional actions if you were not completely successful.

The improvement approach described below, and shown in Figure 2.1, follows similar lines.

1. Consider where there is a need for improvement based on the **results** your organisation aims to achieve. These may concern People, Customers, Partners, Society and Key Performance results. These main stakeholders were discussed in the introduction.

2. Decide what **approaches** need to be implemented or improved in order to achieve your aims. Things are never simple and there is always a variety of options that you may take. A key part of this step is to select the action to be taken.

3. **Deploy** the approaches at an appropriate level in the organisation. This is often more than just communicating

the change and usually involves a change to procedures and behaviours. Change has also to be introduced in a managed way that is culturally acceptable to increase the chances of success.

4. **Assess** and **review** the benefit of the change to ensure that the approaches have been effective. The success of this stage will depend on how well the change was planned and managed.

Figure 2.1 – The Improvement Approach.

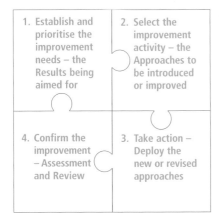

2.2.2 **Step 1: Establish and prioritise the improvement needs – the Results being aimed for**

Whoever gave the advice 'State destination before boarding train' must have had experience of racing off to take action before understanding exactly what the purpose of the action was.

Another trap is to plan to take too much action, which often leads to no action being taken at all. All organisations have limited resources, be these financial and/or human, etc. Therefore it is important to choose to

take action where there is going to be the greatest payback against the chosen objectives.

Even if you think you know what needs to be done this is often based on perception and not fact. The first stage of the improvement process, therefore, is to analyse the current situation and clearly state your aims.

Many methods may be used for this analysis. Organisations that are familiar with the Excellence Model may already be practising 'self-assessment' leading to an abundance of improvement opportunities.

Additionally, you can get an insight from other activities. As part of an organisation's strategic planning activities it may perform regular SWOT analyses that include a review of the organisation's current strengths and weakness as well as a check on the opportunities and threats. Another source could be specific feedback from a stakeholder, such as a customer, or from the results of a benchmarking exercise.

When discussing analysis a key message is that 'you get what you pay for'. An organisation that seeks detailed data on which to make decisions is likely to make better decisions than one that makes decisions just on perceptions or, as is often the case, 'gut feel'. Care should be taken to avoid 'analysis paralysis', however, as things can be taken too far.

Despite these concerns it is important to choose an approach for the analysis that suits the situation. There are many ways of conducting self-assessments against the Excellence Model, including such diverse techniques as a group of managers sitting in a room for a couple of hours to get their view on where they perceive there are gaps, or conducting an 'award' style self-assessment lasting several months that involves collecting lots of data. Both methods are suitable in different situations depending on the purpose of the exercise, which can also be diverse. More detailed explanations of the methods of self-assessment are available from The British Quality Foundation in the publication *How to use the Model*.

The analysis, whichever way it is done, should lead to the point where you may answer several questions. Every organisation will have their own set of questions, but they are likely to include the following:

1. What are the most important over-riding issues that the organisation has to address?

2. Which stakeholders are these issues affecting in a positive way?

3. Are there any stakeholders who will lose out?

4. What is the current performance in this area?

5. By how much must current performance improve to meet targets?

6. What will it take in terms of resource to achieve this level of performance, and can the organisation afford it?

From this list of questions it should be possible to select the priority actions. It should also be possible to screen out any improvements that are outside the organisation's current capabilities, be these market requirements, financial resource requirements, human resource availability or skill availability.

2.2.3 Step 2: Select the improvement activity – the Approaches to be introduced or improved

a. Introduction

It is vital that senior people are on board at this stage, to ensure you have their support for all future actions, as any improvement activities are more likely to occur and be successful if the leaders support them. Therefore, ensure you communicate with your senior people and educate them at all stages of the improvement process.

Rarely is it possible to say 'Yes, that's the action we must take'. In business things are complicated and there are several options that may be followed.

From all the alternatives, it is necessary to choose an option that best suits the results required. This objective should be positive and SMART (Specific, Measurable, Achievable, Realistic and Timely). The following activities may help:

1. Generate options of improvement actions that could be taken.

2. Select the option that describes what is actually going to be done.

3. Define the actual approach or approaches that are to be introduced or improved.

At this stage no consideration is given to how the implementation of the action will be managed, as this is the focus of the next step. You simply concentrate on what needs to be done to achieve the performance that was defined in the first step in terms of the approaches that have to be introduced or improved.

b. **Option generation – what could be done?**

So far all you have is an objective to improve the organisation's performance, but do not know how this will be achieved. Here you can turn to the Excellence Model to generate some options detailing what could be done to reach the required level of performance. However, first you need to understand a bit more about the Excellence Model.

Figure 2.2 – A Basic Form of the Excellence Model.

People manage the organisation's processes that deliver the level of performance. It follows that, if the performance is not at the level required, you can look at either the processes, the way that people are being managed and developed, or a combination of both to find opportunities for improvement. Understanding these linkages turns the Excellence Model into a powerful diagnostic tool.

As you saw in Chapter 1, the full Excellence Model is a little more complicated, but the principles remain the same. The elements show how the drive for Excellence is measured and supported.

The enabler criteria of the Excellence Model are concerned with how the organisation approaches Excellence:

- Leadership – how behaviours/actions support a culture of Excellence.

- Policy and Strategy – how policy and strategy are deployed into plans/actions.

- People – how the organisation releases the potential of its people.

- Partnerships and Resources – how the organisation manages resources effectively/efficiently.

- Processes – how the organisation manages and improves its processes.

The results criteria of the Excellence Model are concerned with what the organisation has achieved and is achieving:

- Customer Results – what is the customer's perception of your organisation and what are your performance indicators in this area?

- People Results – what is the staff's perception of your organisation and what are your performance indicators on this subject?

- Society Results – how does society perceive your organisation and what are your performance indicators on this subject?

- Key Performance Results – what is the organisation achieving in relation to its planned performance?

Table 2.1 – Excellence Model Details.

Criterion	Sub-criteria
1. Leadership How leaders develop and facilitate the achievement of the mission and vision, develop values required for long-term success and implement these via appropriate actions and behaviours, and are personally involved in ensuring the organisation's management system is developed and implemented.	A Leaders develop the mission, vision and values, and are role models of a culture of excellence. B Leaders are personally involved in ensuring the organisation's management system is developed, implemented and continuously improved. C Leaders are involved with customers, partners and representatives of society. D Leaders motivate, support and recognise the organisation's people.
2. Policy and Strategy How the organisation implements its mission and vision via a clear stakeholder-focused strategy, supported by relevant policies, plans, objectives, targets and processes.	A Policy and Strategy are based on the present and future needs and expectations of stakeholders. B Policy and Strategy are based on information from performance measurement, research, learning and creativity related activities. C Policy and Strategy are developed, reviewed and updated. D Policy and Strategy are deployed through a framework of key processes. E Policy and Strategy are communicated and implemented.
3. People How the organisation manages, develops and releases the full potential of its people at an individual, team-based and organisation-wide level, and plans these activities in order to support its policy and strategy and the effective operation of its processes.	A People resources are planned, managed and improved. B People's knowledge and competencies are identified, developed and sustained. C People are involved and empowered. D People and the organisation have a dialogue. E People are rewarded, recognised and cared for.
4. Partnerships and Resources How the organisation plans and manages its external partnerships and internal resources in order to support its policy and strategy and the effective operation of its processes.	A External partnerships are managed. B Finances are managed. C Buildings, equipment and materials are managed. D Technology is managed. E Information and knowledge are managed.
5. Processes How the organisation designs, manages and improves its processes in order to support its policy and strategy and fully satisfy, and generate increasing value for, its customers and other stakeholders.	A Processes are systematically designed and managed. B Processes are improved, as needed, using innovation in order to fully satisfy and generate increasing value for customers and other stakeholders. C Products and services are designed and developed based on customer needs and expectations. D Products and services are produced, delivered and serviced. E Customer relationships are managed and enhanced.

Table 2.1 – Excellence Model Details (continued).

Criterion	Sub-criteria
6. Customer Results What the organisation is achieving in relation to its external customers.	A Perception measures: overall image, products and services, sales and after-sales support, loyalty. B Performance indicators: overall image, products and services, sales and after-sales support, loyalty.
7. People Results What the organisation is achieving in relation to its people.	A Perception measures: motivation, satisfaction. B Performance indicators: achievements, motivation and involvement, satisfaction, services provided to the organisation's people.
8. Society Results What the organisation is achieving in relation to local, national and international society as appropriate.	A Perception measures: performance as a responsible citizen, involvement in the communities where it operates, activities to reduce and prevent nuisance and harm from its operations and/or throughout the life cycle of its products, reporting on activities to assist in the preservation and sustainability of resources. B Performance indicators: handling changes in employment levels, press coverage, dealings with authorities, accolades and awards received.
9. Key Performance Results What the organisation is achieving in relation to its planned performance.	A Key performance outcomes (lag): financial (share price, dividends, gross margin, net profit, sales, meeting of budgets) and non-financial (market share, time to market, volumes, success rates). B Key performance indicators (lead): processes, external resources including partnerships, financial, buildings, equipment and materials, technology, information and knowledge.

The full power of the Excellence Model is realised from the linkages between results and enablers.

Figure 2.3 – The Excellence Model – Starting with Results.

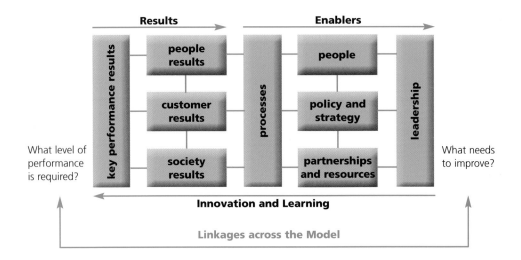

An understanding of the linkages across the Model allows you to identify potential areas for improvement. These linkages may be found at two levels:

1. Across the Model itself between results and enablers, e.g. if there is a need to improve the People Results the key question is where to look for the approaches that could be improved. Figures 2.4–2.7 illustrate these key linkages (based on the work of Diane Dibley in 1999, Information Technology Services Agency, DSS).

2. The second level of linkages is within each criterion, e.g. for Policy and Strategy the sub-criteria follow a logical sequence, and identifying which part of the chain may be weak leads to ideas for improvement. The technical description for each sub-criterion has been given in Table 2.1. Figures 2.8–2.12 detail the linkages between sub-criteria within criteria, and within the set of enablers, using everyday language. There is one figure for each of the five enablers of the Excellence Model.

Figure 2.4 – Linkages between Customer Results and Enablers.

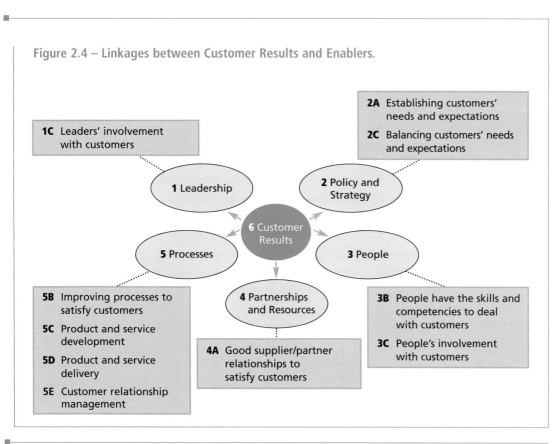

Figure 2.5 – Linkages between People Results and Enablers.

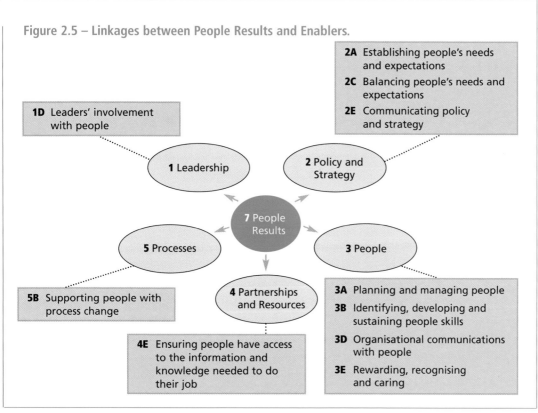

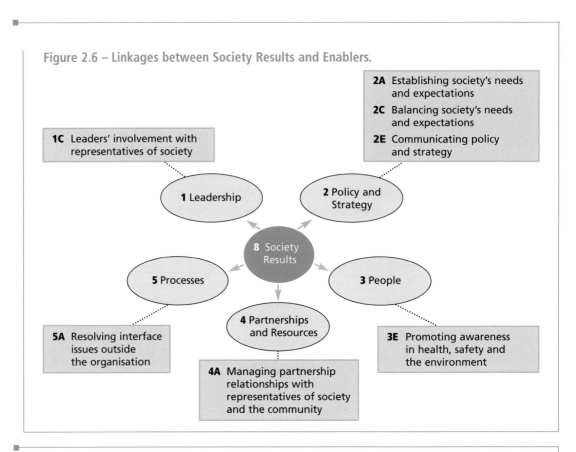

Figure 2.6 – Linkages between Society Results and Enablers.

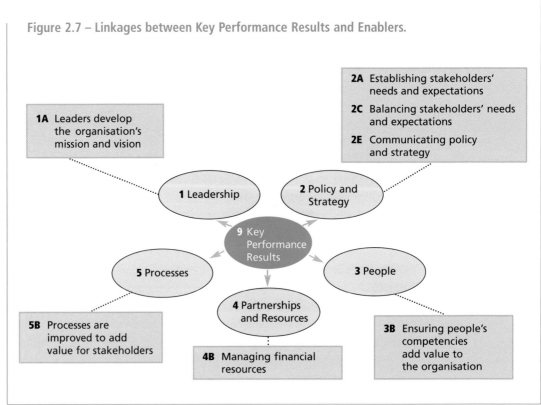

Figure 2.7 – Linkages between Key Performance Results and Enablers.

Figure 2.8 – Linkages within the Leadership Criterion.

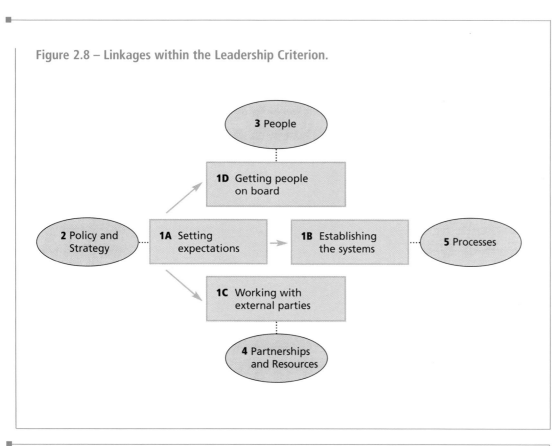

Figure 2.9 – Linkages within the Policy and Strategy Criterion.

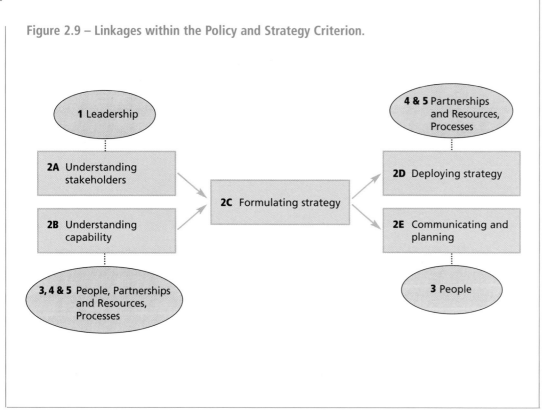

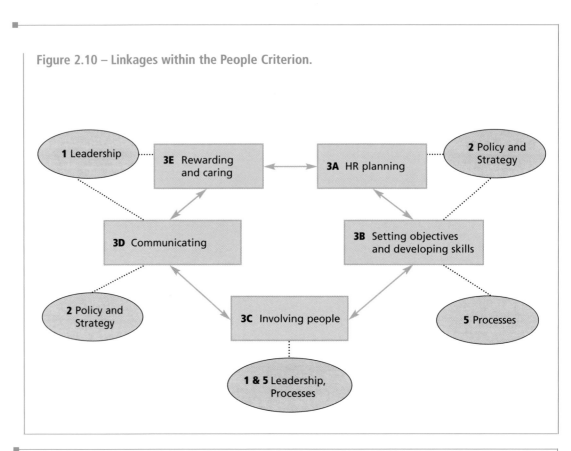

Figure 2.10 – Linkages within the People Criterion.

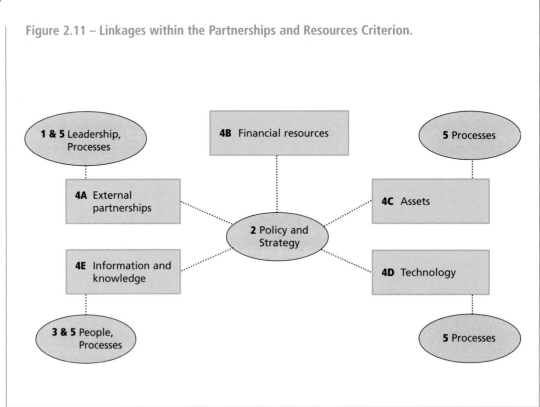

Figure 2.11 – Linkages within the Partnerships and Resources Criterion.

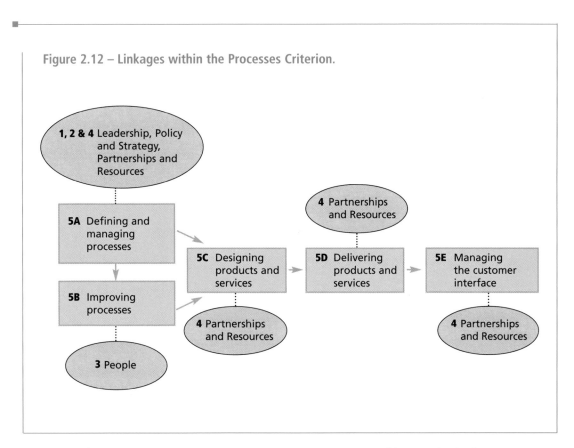

Figure 2.12 – Linkages within the Processes Criterion.

If you want to increase customer satisfaction, you may have identified that your staff are not customer focused, and further investigation may reveal that this is not an issue that training alone will solve. Part of the cause may be the lack of direction or perhaps an inappropriate strategy. The key point here is that you want to open up as many opportunities as possible before deciding what to do.

The reason why these linkages have been presented is as an aid to identifying potential options for improvement action. To use this information it is suggested that you use the following guidance:

1. First review the output from Step 1, where you identified the performance level you are seeking to obtain for a particular stakeholder grouping.

2. Next review Figures 2.4–2.7 by stakeholder grouping to identify sub-criteria that could be targeted for improvement activity.

3. Studying the five enabler figures widens your search for potential improvements by seeing what linkages there are between the particular sub-criterion and linking criteria.

4. Reference to the examples in Chapter 3 will help you understand the detail of each sub-criterion and give you additional ideas.

For example, if your organisation's objective is to increase its performance in customer satisfaction levels from 85 to 90%, refer to Figure 2.4 for Customer Results. This shows the linkages to certain enabler sub-criteria identifying possible areas for you to target for improvement, e.g. it links to 1C – Leaders' involvement with customers. Chapter 3 gives real-life examples of practices that have been carried out under this sub-criterion, and they may either be directly applicable to your organisation or lead to ideas for alternatives.

By the end of your search, you should have many potential areas for improvement activity. The next task in the process is to screen the options so that the most appropriate improvement action may be taken, i.e. prioritise.

c. **Option selection – what are you going to do?**

It is unlikely that there will be only one option as there is always the 'Do nothing' option that should be considered. It is more likely that by this point you will have a short-list of the actions that you could take. It is therefore useful to have simple tools for selecting the chosen action. When taking improvement action there is a cost, in terms of people and money, and a benefit. It is normal that the higher the cost the greater the benefit. However, this is not always the case as simple things can be extremely effective and, if

inappropriate action is chosen, no matter how much effort goes into implementation, the desired performance will not be achieved.

There are several ways to prioritise improvement activities, the detail of which is outside the scope of this book. However, an important point to note at this stage is that if your organisation focuses only on one thing, such as attaining ISO 9000 certification, or gaining Investors in People, there is a chance that something could be missed.

d. **Option design – exactly what needs to be done?**

Working through the previous sections will lead you to a decision on what improvement action you should take. Now is the time to put some more detail on the idea in preparation for implementation in the next step. For example, it may have been decided to introduce an appraisal system, but the question 'How will this work in practice?' has yet to be answered. Process thinking, which is at the heart of the Excellence Model, provides the way forward to achieve this.

Capturing the new or revised approach as a process ensures that all aspects of the improvement can be covered and communicated effectively. In defining the approach the following areas should be covered:

1. What is the aim of the process?

2. What is the scope of the new or revised process? Where does the activity start and where does it end?

3. What is included and what is excluded in the activity?

4. What controls need to be in place to manage the process?

5. Who will operate the approach?

6. What is their required skill and experience level?

7. What equipment and facilities are required?

8. What are the process steps?

9. What measures will be used to monitor the performance of the process?

Use of process mapping and flowcharting is a good way to document the approach and it facilitates communication.

The technique chosen may be based on a widely used approach. Therefore, to help with your improvement planning, Table 2.2 (overleaf) contains a list of some of these approaches, together with a brief description, where they have most impact in the Excellence Model and where to go for more information.

Table 2.2 – Commonly Used Approaches.

Approach	Brief Description	Where it has an impact						Where to go for more information
		← Enabler →						
		1	2	3	4	5	Results	
Activity Based Costing (ABC)	ABC is an approach for assigning overheads to products based on *the way that costs are incurred.* It involves establishing cost pools and cost drivers. The main benefit from the approach is more informed decision-making, but a major concern is the amount of effort required to collect the data on which to base the decisions.				•			Cokins, G., *Activity-Based Cost Management Making It Work: A Manager's Guide to Implementing and Sustaining an Effective ABC System*, Irwin Professional Publications, 1996.
Annual Appraisals and Development Planning	Usually the responsibility of the immediate manager, the approach is used to review past performance targets and translate current year process goals into individual objectives and agree action plans. The approach frequently includes identifying training and development needs. In some approaches, the result of the appraisal is linked to an employee's pay.			•				Knowdell, R.L., *Building a Career Development Program: Nine Steps for Effective Implementation*, Consulting Psychologists Press, 1996.
Balanced Scorecard	First developed by Kaplan and Norton, it recognises the limitations of purely financial measurement of an organisation, which is normally short-term measurement. A scorecard has several measurement perspectives, with the original scorecard having financial, customer, internal business, innovation and learning perspectives. Balanced scorecards are normally a key output from the strategy formulation process.		•					Kaplan, R.S. and Norton, D.P., *The Balanced Scorecard: Translating Strategy into Action*, Harvard Business School Press, Boston (USA), 1996. Neely, A.D, Adams, C. and Kennedy, M., *The Performance Prism: The Scorecard for Measuring and Managing Stakeholder Relationships*, Financial Times/Prentice Hall, 2002. Olve, N.G., et al., *Performance Drivers: A Practical Guide to Using the Balanced Scorecard*, John Wiley and Sons, 1999.
Best Practice Benchmarking	The continuous, systematic search for, and implementation of, best practices that lead to superior performance; it involves comparing performance with leading achievers.	•	•	•	•	•		American Productivity and Quality Center (APQC). BQF Best Practice Benchmarking Studies.

Table 2.2 – Commonly Used Approaches (continued).

| Approach | Brief Description | Where it has an impact
 ← Enabler → | | | | | | Where to go for more information |
		1	2	3	4	5	Results	
								MacDonald, J. and Tanner, S., *Understanding Benchmarking in a Week,* Hodder and Stoughton, 1996. O'Dell, C.S., et al., *If Only We Knew What We Know: The Transfer of Internal Knowledge and Best Practice,* Free Press, 1998.
Business Process Re-engineering (BPR)	The fundamental re-think and re-design of a business process, its structure and associated management systems to deliver major or step improvements in performance.				•			Hunt, V.D. and Hunt, D.V., *Process Mapping: How to Re-engineer Your Business Processes,* John Wiley and Sons, 1996. Hammer, M. and Champy, J., *Re-engineering the Corporation: A Manifesto for Business Revolution,* HarperBusiness, New York, 1993. Miller, L.C.E., *Business Process Re-engineering: A Management Guidebook* (2nd Edition), Vertical Systems, Inc., 1996.
Charter Mark Framework	Government award scheme for recognising and encouraging excellence in public service. It concentrates on results – the service the customer actually receives, putting the users first, and delivering a first-class service.				•		•	Publications and leaflets, e.g. *Charter Mark, Guide for Applicants and Why You Should Apply,* are available from the Charter Unit Publications Line on 0845 722 3242.
Communication Strategies	As part of the organisation's overall policy and strategy, clearly defined guidelines for ensuring effective vertical and horizontal communications in all media, both within the organisation and externally. It is reviewed, updated and improved periodically, based on feedback from stakeholders.	•	•	•	•	•		Hodgdon, L.A., *Visual Strategies for Improving Communication,* Quirk Roberts Publishing,1995.

Table 2.2 – Commonly Used Approaches (continued).

Approach	Brief Description	1	2	3	4	5	Results	Where to go for more information
			Where it has an impact ← Enabler →					
Competitive Benchmarking	The identification of external comparison data such that an organisation's performance relative to its competitors may be determined.		•			•	•	Bendell, T., et al., *Benchmarking for Competitive Advantage* (2nd Edition), Financial Times Management, 1997. Boxwell R.J., Jr., *Benchmarking for Competitive Advantage*, McGraw-Hill, 1993. Camp, R.C., *Business Process Benchmarking; finding and implementing best practice*, ASQC Quality Press, Milwaukee, WI (USA), 1995.
Cost of Quality Measurement	The concept was introduced to focus senior management attention on the cost of quality problems. In doing this it promoted the need for quality in a language they could understand. Two factors are normally considered – the cost of non-conformance, e.g. the cost of the rectification of defects or scrap and a cost associated with lost business, and the cost of quality, which covers the cost of all the activities that aim to prevent a quality failure. These include prevention, appraisal and training costs.					•	•	Dale, B.G. and Plunkett, J.J., *Quality Costings*, Chapman and Hall, London, 1991. Hronec, S.M., *Vital Signs: Using Quality, Time and Cost Performance Measurements to Chart Your Company's Future*, Amacom, 1993. Payson, S., *Quality Measurement in Economics: New Perspectives on the Evolution of Goods and Services*, Edward Elgar Publications, 1994
Deming's Plan-Do-Check-Act Cycle	Deming's cycle of continuous improvement – Plan-Do-Check-Act.		•					Deming, W.E., *Out of the Crisis*, MIT, Cambridge, Mass., (USA), 1982. Walton, M. and Deming, W.E., *Deming Management Method*, Perigee, 1998.

Table 2.2 – Commonly Used Approaches (continued).

Approach	Brief Description	Where it has an impact ← Enabler →						Where to go for more information
		1	2	3	4	5	Results	
Employee Surveys	These are used to gather information from employees about their needs, expectations and satisfaction. There are many ways to collect the information, including: focus groups, questionnaires, workshops, interviews, telephone and e-mail. The results should be analysed, publicised and responded to.	•	•				•	Folkman, J. and Zenger, J., *Employee Surveys That Make A Difference: Using Customised Feedback Tools to Transform Your Organisation,* Executive Excellence, 1999. Kraut, A.I., and Kraut, A J, *Organisational Surveys: Tools for Assessment and Change (Social and Behavioural Science)* Jossey-Bass, 1996.
Failure Mode, Effect and Criticality Analysis (FMECA)	Processes can be analysed to determine possible modes of failure and their effects on the performance of the product or operation. FMECA is the study of potential failures to determine their effects, with results ranked in order of seriousness.				•			Dorner, D., et al., *The Logic of Failure: Recognising and Avoiding Error in Complex Situations,* Perseus Press, 1997. Stamatis, D.H., *Failure Mode and Effect Analysis: FMEA from Theory to Execution,* AMER Society for Quality, 1995.
Flowcharting	A graphical method used to record the detail of processes by showing them as a series of tasks and activities using standard symbols. Use is normally made of software to draw the diagrams.				•			Boillot, M.H., et al., *Essentials of Flowcharting,* WCB/McGraw-Hill, 1995.
HASAW	The Health and Safety at Work Act (HASAW) seeks to secure the health, safety and welfare of persons at work, for protecting others against risks to health or safety in connection with the activities of persons at work, for controlling the keeping and use and preventing the unlawful acquisition, possession and use of dangerous substances, and for controlling certain emissions to the atmosphere.		•	•				Diberardinis, L.J., *Handbook of Occupational Safety and Health,* John Wiley and Sons, 1998. Woodside, G., *Environmental, Health and Safety Portable Handbook,* McGraw-Hill, 1998.

Table 2.2 – Commonly Used Approaches (continued).

Approach	Brief Description	Where it has an impact ← Enabler →						Where to go for more information
		1	2	3	4	5	Results	
IDEFO (Integration Definition Function Modelling)	A structured graphical framework for describing and improving business processes based on an approach developed by the American armed forces. A model consists of a hierarchical series of diagrams, text and glossary, cross-referenced through boxes (process components) and arrows (data and objects).					•		Barker, R. and Longman, C., *Case Method: Function and Process Modelling*, Addison-Wesley Publishing Company, 1992. De Carteret, C. and Vidgen, R., *Data Modelling for Information Systems*, Financial Times Management, 1995.
Investors in People (IIP)	A UK National Standard that sets a level of good practice for training and development of people to achieve business goals. The Investors in People certificate is awarded to organisations that pass an external assessment.		•					Gilliland, N., *Developing Your Business Through Investors in People*, Gower Publishing Company, 1997.
ISO 9000 Based Quality Management Systems	It sets out how the methods incorporating all the activities associated with quality in an organisation are implemented to ensure that the performance requirements and needs of the customer are fully met.			•	•	•		British Standards Institution: *ISO/CDI 9001:2000 Quality Management Systems*. Hoyle, D., *ISO9000 Pocket Guide*, Butterworth-Heinemann, 1998. Rothery, B., *ISO9000*, Gower Publications Company.
ISO 14000	A specification for environmental management systems for ensuring and demonstrating compliance *with stated policies and objectives*. It can enable any organisation to establish an effective management system as a foundation for sound environmental performance and participation in environmental auditing schemes. It is now possible to undergo a third party audit and receive a certificate of compliance.				•	•		British Standards Institution. Block, M.R. and Marash, I.R., *Integrating ISO4001 into a Quality Management System*, AMER Society for Quality, 2000. Tanner, D. and Bellamy, R., *Environmental Management in Asia: A Guide to ISO14000*, AET Limited, 1997.

Table 2.2 – Commonly Used Approaches (continued).

Approach	Brief Description	Where it has an impact ◄— Enabler —►						Where to go for more information
		1	2	3	4	5	Results	
JIT (Just-in-Time)	Concerns the delivery of materials to manufacturing locations at the point that they are required for production. The emphasis is on increased efficiency and reduction in waste, shortening of lead times, improvement in quality, continuous improvement and simplicity.				•	•		Hirano, H. and Hiroyuki, H., *JIT Factory Revolution: A Pictorial Guide to Factory Design of the Future*, Productivity Press, 1989. Petroff, J.N., *Handbook of MRP III/JIT Integration and Implementation*, Prentice Hall, 1993.
Job Descriptions	Used to define the requirements of a specific job and as a reference for recruitment. They should contain, as a minimum, activities to be undertaken in performing the job and requirements of the individual in terms of experience, skills and training.		•					Plachy, R.J., *Results Orientated Job Descriptions: More Than 225 Models to Use or Adapt – With Guidelines for Creating Your Own*, Amacom, 1993. Plachy, S.J. and Plachy, R.J., *More Results – Orientated Job Descriptions: 226 Models to Use or Adapt – With Guidelines for Creating Your Own*, Amacom, 1998.
Leadership Assessment and 360° Appraisal	Assessment of a leader's performance against established leadership criteria. Data is normally collected through surveying a leader's superiors, peers and direct staff.	•		•				Edwards, M.R. and Ewen, A.J. (Contributor), *360 Degree Feedback: The Powerful New Model for Employee Assessment and Performance Improvement*, Amacom, 1996. Humphrey, B. and Stokes, J., *The 21st Century Supervisor: Self Assessment – Nine Essential Skills for Developing Frontline Leaders*, Jossey-Bass, 1999.

Table 2.2 – Commonly Used Approaches (continued).

Approach	Brief Description	Where it has an impact ← Enabler →						Where to go for more information
		1	2	3	4	5	Results	
Market Surveys and Customer Observations	These are used to acquire information about customer needs and expectations, which informs policy and strategy and is used as a basis for product and service development. There are several types and the right mix is essential to ensure the correct information is gathered.		•			•		Jarboe, G.R., *The Marketing Research Project Manual*, West Wadsworth, 1996. Wing, M.J., et al., *The Arthur Andersen Guide to Talking With Your Customers: What They Will Tell You About Your Business: When You Ask the Right Questions*, Upstart Publishing Company, 1977.
Materials Requirement Planning II (MRP II)	Requirement Planning is a set of techniques that uses bill of materials, inventory on hand and on order, and the production schedule or plan to calculate the quantities and timing of materials. MRPII is a computer-based system that arose from an appreciation of the need to time and phase materials with resource availability so as to achieve a given output date.			•	•			Oden, H.W., et al., *Handbook of Material* and *Capacity Requirements Planning*, McGraw-Hill, 1993. Orlicky, J. and Plossl, G.W., *Orlicky's Material Requirements Planning*, McGraw-Hill, 1994.
Policy Deployment (or Goal Translation) Process	This identifies how to achieve the mission, i.e. translate the 'what's' into 'how's', right through the organisation.		•	•				Alai, Y., *Hoshin Kanri: Policy Deployment for Successful TQM*, Productivity Press, 1991. Sheridan, B.M., *Policy Deployment: The TQM Approach to Long-Range Planning*, AMER, Society for Quality, 1993.
Political, Economic, Social, Technology, Legal, Environmental (PESTLE) Analysis	Identifying and understanding political, economic, demographic, social, technological, legal and environmental issues and their effect on the organisation's policy and strategy.		•					Johnson, G. and Scholes, K., *Exploring Corporate Strategy* (6th Edition), Prentice Hall Europe, 2002.

Table 2.2 – Commonly Used Approaches (continued).

Approach	Brief Description	Where it has an impact Enabler					Results	Where to go for more information
		1	2	3	4	5		
Prioritisation of Improvement	The use of simple tools to assist in the prioritisation of defined improvement opportunities, taking into account the level of benefit and the amount of effort required. The ideal improvement activity will have a high impact on the organisation for a low investment in resource, financial investment or need to overcome resistance.				•			Oakland, J.S., *Total Organisational Excellence – Achieving World Class Performance,* (Revised Paperback Edn.), Butterworth-Heinemann, 2001. Oakland, J.S., *Total Quality Management – The Route to Improving Performance* (2nd Edition), Butterworth-Heinmann, 1993.
Process Mapping/Modelling	Using simple flowcharts or more advanced techniques such as IDEF0 to describe what a process does, what it controls, what things it works on, what means it uses to perform its functions and what it produces. Process modelling involves the creation of 'What if' scenarios as a part of improvement activities such as Business Process Re-engineering (BPR).				•			Damelio, R., *The Basics of Process Mapping,* Productivity Inc., 1996. Hunt, V.D., and Hunt, D.V., *Process Mapping: How to Re-engineer Your Business Processes,* John Wiley and Sons, 1996. Scholz-Reiter, B. and Stickel, E., *Business Process Modelling,* Springer Verlag, 1996.
Project Management	There are many approaches to managing projects but they all involve balancing the scope of the change (how much is achieved) and quality of the change (how well it is achieved) against how much it costs and how long it takes. Project management includes a variety of tools and techniques such as Project Definitions, Project Plans and Gantt Charts.				•			Cleland, D.I. and King, W.R., *Project Management Handbook,* John Wiley and Sons, 1988. Anderson, E.S., Grude, K. V. and Haug, T., *Goal Directed Project Management,* Kogan Page, 1998. Turner, J.R., *The Handbook of Project-Based Management,* McGraw-Hill, 1993.

Table 2.2 – Commonly Used Approaches (continued).

Approach	Brief Description	Where it has an impact ← Enabler →						Where to go for more information
		1	2	3	4	5	Results	
Psychometric Tests	Methods to assess an individual's behaviour and preferences by getting them to complete a questionnaire where they have to rate a series of statements. Two of the better-known tests are FIRO-B (Fundamental Interpersonal Relationship Orientation Behaviour) Instrument and the Myers-Briggs Type Indicator. The first looks at the dynamics of relationships and the second is a tool for team development.	•		•				Nunnally, J.C. and Bernstein, I.H., *Psychometric Theory* (McGraw-Hill Series in Social Psychology), McGraw-Hill College Division, 1994. Parkinson, M., *How to Master Psychometric Tests: Winning Strategies for Test Takers,* Kogan Page Ltd, 1998.
Quality Function Deployment (QFD)	A technique to compare the technical or operating characteristics of a product or service with customer needs. A multi-disciplinary team carries it out.					•		Cohen, L. and Cohen, L., *Quality Function Deployment: How to Make QFD Work for You (Engineering Process Improvement),* Addison-Wesley Publications Company, 1995. Revelle, J.B., et al., *The QFD Handbook,* John Wiley and Sons, 1998.
Six Sigma	The number of standard deviations from the average setting of a process to the tolerance limit. In statistical terms, this translates to 3.4 defects per million. 'Six Sigma' has become an approach to managing the output of manufacturing operations to ensure high levels of quality.					•		BQF Six Sigma Service Breyfogle, F.W., *Implementing Six Sigma: Smarter Solutions Using Statistical Methods,* John Wiley and Sons, 1999. Harry, M.J. and Schrodeder, R., *Six Sigma: The Breakthrough Management Strategy Revolutionising The World's Top Corporations,* Doubleday, 1999.

Table 2.2 – Commonly Used Approaches (continued).

Approach	Brief Description	Where it has an impact ← Enabler →						Where to go for more information
		1	2	3	4	5	Results	
Stakeholder Analysis	A way of analysing which stakeholders need to be managed when trying to manage change. Stakeholders, who can be internal or external, have a level of interest and a degree of power, e.g. stakeholders with high levels of interest in any change and who possess high levels of power need to be carefully managed. Other stakeholders may only need to be kept informed.		•	•		•		Johnson, G. and Scholes, K., *Exploring Corporate Strategy* (6th Edition), Prentice Hall Europe, 2002.
Statistical Process Control (SPC)	Measurement of the output of a process at regular intervals. A simple mathematical calculation allows the determination of the quality level of the output. When plotted on a 'Control Chart', it is possible to differentiate the expected 'normal causes' of variation from 'special causes' of variation, which signal a problem with the process. The Control Chart also allows the process to be monitored over time and thereby the forecasting of future potential quality problems.					•		Abbott, J.C., *Practical Understanding of Capability by Implementing Statistical Process Control*, SPC (3rd Edition), Robert Houston Smith Publisher, 1999. Oakland, J.S., *Statistical Process Control: A Practical Guide* (4th Edition), Butterworth-Heinemann, 1999. Quesenberry, C.P., *SPC Methods for Quality Improvement*, John Wiley and Sons,1997.
Strengths, Weaknesses, Opportunities, Threats (SWOT) Analysis	A method for identifying current strengths and weaknesses within the organisation and future potential opportunities and threats.		•					Johnson, G. and Scholes, K, *Exploring Corporate Strategy* (6th Edition), Prentice Hall Europe, 2002.
Suggestion Schemes	A method for employees to propose ideas for improvement within the organisation by a number of routes, sometimes anonymously, using boxes placed around the workplace, or via their line manager, either informally or formally. The management considers all suggestions and responses are publicised.			•		•		Martin, C.L., and Bassford, R., (Contributor), *Employee Suggestion Systems: Boosting Productivity and Profits (Fifty-Minute Series)*, Crisp Publishing, 1997.

Table 2.2 – Commonly Used Approaches (continued).

Approach	Brief Description	Where it has an impact Enabler					Results	Where to go for more information
		1	2	3	4	5		
Supplier Partnerships	The philosophy is that, through co-operation, rather than confrontation, both parties benefit. It is a longer-term view, emphasising total cost rather than product price. Long-term, stable relationships are sought rather than short-term quick advantage transactions.	•			•			Hale, R.L., *Managing Supplier Quality: How to Develop Customer-Supplier Partnerships That Work*, Monochrome Press, 1994. Stimson, *J.A., Supplier Partnerships (The Purchasing Excellence Series)*, Pt Publishing, 1999.
Total Productive Maintenance (TPM)	An approach developed in Japan to involve production workers in the maintenance of their own equipment such that manufacturing becomes more productive. Based on a 'six pillars' concept that includes training and continuous improvement as well as maintenance, the approach also has the benefit of increasing people involvement and team working.			•		•		Willmott, P., *Total Productive Maintenance: The Western Way*, Butterworth-Heinemann, 1995.
Total Quality Management (TQM)	Total Quality Management (TQM) is far wider in its application than just assuring product or service quality – it is a way of managing people and business processes to ensure complete customer satisfaction at every stage, internally and externally.	•		•	•	•		Choppin, J., *Quality Through People: A Blueprint for Proactive Total Quality Management*, Rushmere Wynne, Bedford (UK), 1997. Crampa, D.,*Total Quality – A User's Guide for Implementation*, Addison-Wesley, Reading, MA, USA, 1992. Oakland, J.S., *TQM – Text with Cases* (2nd Edition), Butterworth-Heinemann, 2000.

2.2.4 Step 3: Take action – Deploying the new or revised approaches

So far you have established what level of performance is required and what action you believe needs to be taken to deliver this level of performance. Now is the time to take the action.

It is considered good practice to define the change using a project brief or terms of reference. This document builds on the definition of the aims of the change that were developed in Step 1. For small changes these can be quite brief documents and may include entries such as:

- The aim of the change together with performance objectives/ success measures.

- Scope of the change – what is included and what is outside the improvement activity, e.g. the improvement may be only deployed in one area of the organisation or at one organisational level.

- What benefits will be delivered as a result of the change and when will they be delivered?

- What the estimated cost of the change will be and over what time-frame.

- Who will be affected by the change, in both a positive and negative sense?

Not only does the project definition provide clarity over what is to be achieved, it also acts as a reference document that may be referred back to once the change is complete. Such a document also allows changes to the project to be implemented in a controlled way.

When implementing change it is important to recognise that it is not a good idea to simply announce the change, take the action and then expect that the improved performance will be maintained. Before taking the improvement action it is essential to get people on board and to spend time explaining why the change is necessary and that it is not a one-off exercise. The change will be made to meet future objectives and it is important to point out that more change will probably follow.

It is crucial to do this with the people the change will affect. The examples contained in Chapter 3 of this book can be used to explain what other organisations are doing as a way of educating people regarding change. They may also be used to overcome barriers and to show what is possible.

Once the change has been implemented action is often necessary to make the change stick, e.g. organisations may change their reward and remuneration policies to encourage certain behaviours and to make sure that old habits do not return.

Preparing a simple project plan will be a worthwhile investment to manage the changes in a controlled way. Any change has to balance three factors:

- What is achieved – the quality of the output.

- What it costs – what resource is required.

- What time – how long it will take.

- To what extent was the scope of the project achieved? For example, to what extent was the detail of the project delivered and what was the quality of the outcome?

These factors are often traded against each other as an organisation seeks to implement the best solution in the shortest time possible and at minimal cost. Lengthening the timescale of a project to improve the output almost always increases the cost.

There are many tools and techniques that can be used to manage the balance of these three factors, a description of which is outside the scope of this book. Useful references for further information have been included in Table 2.2.

2.2.5 **Step 4: Confirm the improvement – Assessment and Review**

A key benefit from producing a project brief is that it provides a useful reference against which to determine the success of the improvement action. If the original aims have been achieved then the action may be closed. If not, it might be necessary to return to Step 2 and generate some more options for improvement activity.

Whatever the outcome of the assessment against the original aims, it is useful to conduct a 'Post-Completion Review' to record what has been learnt and how change may be handled more effectively in the future. Typical questions for a post-completion review include:

- Were the aims and objectives achieved?

- Did the project deliver on time?

- How did the actual cost compare with the estimated cost?

- How well was the team working?

- What went well?

- What could be improved? For example, were there any problems that could have been avoided?

- How was the project team perceived by the stakeholders in terms of how it delivered the project?

2.3 Summary

The aim of this chapter was to present a simple approach for improving the performance of your organisation based on RADAR. The approach includes several aspects of change management, including the need to establish clear objectives for the change, selecting the most appropriate actions and project managing the change.

The examples that follow in Chapter 3 may be used for many purposes, including as a source of information to stimulate ideas on what areas to improve. In addition, they also support the change process by using them:

- To educate people and communicate the approaches.

- To overcome barriers by demonstrating what is actually possible.

- To promote Excellence to all stakeholder groups, be these shareholders, customers, partners, society or people.

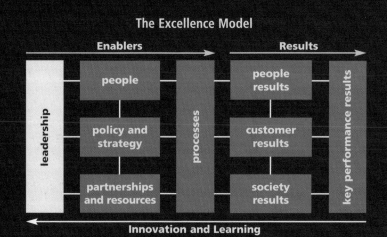

The Excellence Model

Enablers

Results

leadership

people

policy and
strategy

partnerships
and resources

processes

people
results

customer
results

society
results

key performance results

Innovation and Learning

© 1999 EFQM.

Chapter 3 | Practical Examples

Criterion 1

"Leaders set the organisation's direction, a plan for getting there, ensure all employees are on board and are involved with key stakeholders."

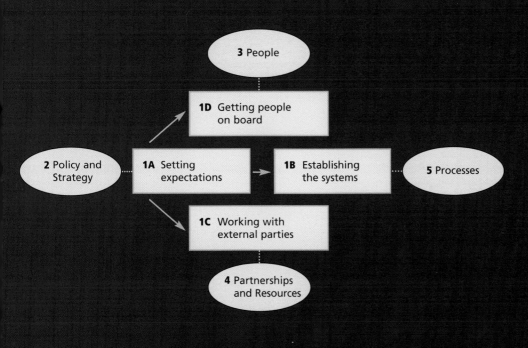

Linkages between the sub-criteria and with the other enablers

3.1 Leadership

How leaders develop and facilitate the achievement of the mission and vision, develop values required for long-term success and implement these via appropriate actions and behaviours, and are personally involved in ensuring that the organisation's management system is developed and implemented.

Sub-criterion 1A:

Leaders develop the mission, vision and values and are role models of a culture of excellence.

Areas to address may include:

- *Developing the organisation's mission and vision;*

- *Developing and role modelling ethics and values that support the creation of the organisation's culture;*

- *Reviewing and improving the effectiveness of their own leadership and acting upon future leadership requirements;*

- *Being personally and actively involved in improvement activities;*

- *Stimulating and encouraging empowerment, creativity and innovation;*

- *Encouraging, supporting and acting upon the findings of learning activities;*

- *Prioritising improvement activities;*

- *Stimulating and encouraging collaboration within the organisation.*

PRIVATE SECTOR

Each year our vision is reviewed as part of our annual performance review and planning process to ensure it remains our guiding principle and helps identify our business priorities.

Our Executive team emphasize the importance they place on 'living the values' and devised the 'value driven change' programme. Under this programme the vision and values were used to test the validity of all actions underlining all our behaviours that would take us towards the goal of becoming world-class. Each senior manager from the Managing Director downwards, owns and leads value-driven action or actions.

Our Executive team lead through example by always being the first group to be trained when each new improvement initiative is introduced to strengthen sections of the Excellence Model. The leadership effectiveness of our managers is assessed through the performance planning review (PPR).

The individual manager's strengths and objectives for improvement are identified and reviewed with their line manager as part of their annual assessment. We reinforce and sustain our approach to leadership by all our managers going through 360-degree personal feedback reviews.

Our managers have successfully led the company-wide deployment of quality initiatives such as ISO 9002, Charter Mark, ISO14001 and Investors in People. To date our Executive team have participated in Quality Improvement Teams, as sponsors, leaders or team members, covering over 300 projects.

We train our managers in the skills required to support their teams and use a cascade approach to communications to ensure accessibility and common understanding through two-way interaction.

Links to Fundamental Concepts

☑ Leadership and constancy of purpose	☐ Customer focus
☐ Management by process and facts	☐ Partner development
☑ People development and involvement	☐ Public responsibility
☐ Continuous learning, improvement and innovation	☐ Results orientation

Criterion 1

The organisation reviewed its Mission, Vision and Values and agreed on statements that underpin the work of the Department. These statements influence how we approach the work we do and how we deal with people inside and outside the Agency.

There have been calls for a radical change in culture, service and approach so that assessments are calculated quickly and accurately. In preparation we have ensured that all leaders have the skills and knowledge to do their job by developing and delivering a comprehensive Management Development Programme and Foundation Management Programme.

The programme, completed in partnership with the University of Ulster at Jordanstown, included learning and development, mentoring and Myers Briggs profiling. It was first delivered to middle managers and following extensive evaluation and review it was rolled out to first line managers. A member of Agency Management Board opens each Induction event and a senior manager is present at each workshop.

The effectiveness of leadership is monitored, evaluated and reviewed through our Performance Review System and also when performance is measured.

Our Corporate Governance Framework document lists the roles and responsibilities of each board member, the post responsibility, the corporate responsibilities and the leadership and management ethos required of each board member.

Roles and responsibilities are cascaded to all other managers at the appropriate level and formulate the basis of the Performance Review System.

Senior leaders reviewed and improved the effectiveness of leadership through attendance at the Civil Service College.

The Managing Director formed the company in 1990 with a vision 'to be the best moulding manufacturer'. From this vision he developed a mission by 1993 that focuses on continual improvement and customer satisfaction.

This family have brought to the business certain values, which have provided a solid foundation for their family life. These values are integrity, loyalty, respect and working together as a team and they are an inherent part of the company.

The partnerships that the Managing Director has built with employees, customers, suppliers and support agencies have flourished and loyalty has strengthened with our ability to nurture these values in all the new partnerships that are formed.

All employees and external organisations appreciate our integrity and respect for their views that we use in our dealings with them.

The effectiveness of the leadership of the Executive Team/Management Team is reviewed twice yearly through Personal Development Plans.

In 1997 at his Personal Development Plan review the Production Manager asked the Managing Director to take a step back and allow him to take full control of the factory floor. The Managing Director did as requested and over the following years increasingly moved into a more managerial rather than hands on role in all areas of the business. The Director Business Excellence has also increasingly given over all human resource issues to the Human Resource Manager since their appointment in 1999.

The two directors now concentrate on the future needs of the business and spend time identifying best practice organizations and learning from them.

Links to Fundamental Concepts

☑ Leadership and constancy of purpose

☐ Management by process and facts

☑ People development and involvement

☐ Continuous learning, improvement and innovation

☐ Customer focus

☐ Partner development

☐ Public responsibility

☐ Results orientation

Links to Fundamental Concepts

☑ Leadership and constancy of purpose

☐ Management by process and facts

☑ People development and involvement

☑ Continuous learning, improvement and innovation

☑ Customer focus

☑ Partner development

☐ Public responsibility

☐ Results orientation

Criterion 1

3.1 Leadership

How leaders develop and facilitate the achievement of the mission and vision, develop values required for long-term success and implement these via appropriate actions and behaviours, and are personally involved in ensuring the organisation's management system is developed and implemented.

Sub-criterion 1B:
Leaders are personally involved in ensuring the organisation's management system is developed, implemented and continuously improved.

Areas to address may include:

- *Aligning the organisation's structure to support delivery of its policy and strategy;*

- *Ensuring a system for managing processes is developed and implemented;*

- *Ensuring a process for the development, deployment and updating of policy and strategy is developed and implemented;*

- *Ensuring a process for the measurement, review and improvement of key results is developed and implemented;*

- *Ensuring a process, or processes, for stimulating, identifying, planning and implementing improvements to enabling approaches, e.g. through creativity, innovation and learning activities, is developed and implemented.*

PRIVATE SECTOR

A five element 'Management System' has been defined by leaders that demonstrates how the top-level strategic goals are realised through a process management model. This framework has been developed at the most senior leadership level of the business.

The first element, 'The Way We Lead', is the definition of the goals using a framework that details how the growth of the business will be achieved through the delivery of six strategic themes. These include a statement on the required culture and operational improvements such as Supply Chain efficiency. Each strategic theme has a set of clear goals.

The second element is the business model for the organisation and this defines 'The Way We Work'. Reviewed and refined through many cycles, this business model represents all the activities of the business. This element is followed by the 'The Way We Measure Progress' element, where the current performance is compared with the planned performance. This element includes the use of self-assessment in a diagnostic way to identify the drivers that are required to meet the required levels of performance.

The fourth and fifth elements relate to managing change. 'The Way We Transform' features the approach to organisation re-design and 'The Way We Develop People' to the way that the leaders and the desired culture of the future are developed.

Links to Fundamental Concepts

☑ Leadership and constancy of purpose	☐ Customer focus
☑ Management by process and facts	☐ Partner development
	☐ Public responsibility
☑ People development and involvement	☐ Results orientation
☐ Continuous learning, improvement and innovation	

Criterion 1

PUBLIC SECTOR

Foreign language teaching is not obligatory at primary level. However, striving for continual excellence we have an action plan for European languages to be taught from the age of 6 years old. The Headteacher was committed to the idea of teaching a second language to children as young as possible.

- The Headteacher ensured that the Governing body realized the importance of a child learning a foreign language early in their education.
- The teaching staff discussed the principle of teaching a second language and felt that it would be a very good idea as it would augment our English teaching by giving children a greater understanding of 'parts of speech'.
- The Governors incorporated the idea in their School Improvement and Development Plan.
- A language teacher was appointed to teach French to the oldest class, 10/11 years old. It was decided to keep the lessons primarily oral and fun. The emphasis being on communicating in French, using colloquial French, which they could use on holiday.
- The teachers and parents appraised the results. They found that:
  - The parents were very pleased that their children were being taught a second language.
  - The children were pleased to learn a language but were embarrassed to speak in another language.
- At the Governors' annual planning meeting in July it was agreed to continue with the French teaching but to begin a little earlier to see if the embarrassment of speaking a second language could be lessened. The School Improvement Development Plan reflected a determination on behalf of the Governors to develop a growing awareness of European studies in its 5-year plan.
- The teaching staff under the direction of the French teacher drew up a French policy. French was taught to the 2 oldest classes – ages from 8 to 11 years. The local secondary school agreed to monitor our children's progress in French during their first year there.

Links to Fundamental Concepts

- ☑ Leadership and constancy of purpose
- ☑ Management by process and facts
- ☐ People development and involvement
- ☐ Continuous learning, improvement and innovation
- ☑ Customer focus
- ☐ Partner development
- ☐ Public responsibility
- ☐ Results orientation

SMALL/MEDIUM

Policy and strategy are implemented and delivered through a suite of key processes which are subject to systematic monitoring, review and improvement through regular meetings at which both leaders and staff attend. These meetings range in frequency and formality. Every morning at 9:30, we all take coffee together, which provides an informal opportunity to review the events (both business and social) of the previous day and look forward to the current day. On a more formal basis we hold a Weekly Sales meeting every Friday, which all colleagues attend. There is a set, structured agenda for these meetings and their main focus is to review sales volumes against plan and, where there are negative variances, to discuss and agree necessary corrective action.

However, the main vehicle for ensuring that policies and strategies are realised via a range of key processes is our Monthly Quality Management Review Meeting at which all staff do their utmost to attend. The purpose and format of these monthly meetings has evolved over time and after discussion between the Managing Director and his colleagues. We believe that effective process management is the key to "getting things done well".

We are ISO 9002 certified and have been since 1994. Our Human Resources process conforms to the Investors in People standards and we have been IiP certified since 1996. We believe that Processes are the link between business objectives and strategies and the achievement of results, which satisfy all stakeholders. Each member of staff owns processes relevant to their area of responsibility. Each process is reviewed on a monthly, quarterly, six monthly or annual basis, according to how critical they are to achieving our policy and strategy. Performance of processes against targets is reviewed at the MQMRM.

Links to Fundamental Concepts

- ☑ Leadership and constancy of purpose
- ☑ Management by process and facts
- ☐ People development and involvement
- ☐ Continuous learning, improvement and innovation
- ☐ Customer focus
- ☐ Partner development
- ☐ Public responsibility
- ☐ Results orientation

Criterion 1

3.1 Leadership

How leaders develop and facilitate the achievement of the mission and vision, develop values required for long-term success and implement these via appropriate actions and behaviours, and are personally involved in ensuring the organisation's management system is developed and implemented.

Sub-criterion 1C:
Leaders are involved with customers, partners and representatives of society.

Areas to address may include:

- *Meeting, understanding and responding to needs and expectations;*

- *Establishing and participating in partnerships;*

- *Establishing and participating in joint improvement activity;*

- *Recognising individuals and teams of stakeholders for their contribution to the business, for loyalty etc;*

- *Participating in professional bodies, conferences and seminars, particularly promoting and supporting Excellence;*

- *Supporting and engaging in activities that aim to improve the environment and the organisation's contribution to society.*

PRIVATE SECTOR

The divisional ring fence supported by the Customer Satisfaction Survey is used to determine our key interfaces. Where key partnerships are identified, the process of 'Building Business Partnerships' is implemented. Use of the process is at the discretion of the general managers and forms a key element of the 'Challenge of Leadership' programme.

Two of our managers ensure that our policy of Building Business Partnerships, with the objectives of doubling the Customer Satisfaction Index and halving flight line complaints, is understood throughout our organisation. Our 200 leaders are playing the major role in achieving these stretch targets and to emphasise our intent we invited seven of our customers to participate in a process management workshop. Each paired with one of our managers to address the corporate company strategy of establishing better process control. Prior to close of the workshop each pairing formulated an action plan aimed at strengthening working relationships.

This partnering lead has been cascaded through our organisation. Our customers are highly complimentary and the strong partnerships form solid foundations for the future.

We have weekly business reviews with managing directors of the Operating Business Units who supply the components and parts we assemble into engines. Delivery performance, quality and cost are monitored to ensure components are delivered to the engine build line at the contracted date. A quarterly forum for all our managers provides a mechanism to receive customers' and suppliers' input.

Links to Fundamental Concepts

☑ Leadership and constancy of purpose	☑ Customer focus
	☑ Partner development
☐ Management by process and facts	☐ Public responsibility
	☐ Results orientation
☐ People development and involvement	
☐ Continuous learning, improvement and innovation	

Criterion 1

PUBLIC SECTOR

Leaders regularly meet our stakeholders and their representatives and the feedback we receive is used in the development of Policy and Strategy. The purpose of these meetings is to identify and address stakeholder needs and to use this feedback in the development of Policy and Strategy. We introduced Face-to-Face contact to ensure customers have direct contact with staff when they request it.

Closer Working with the Benefits Agency provides a more unified service. We have extended the service so that the Benefits Agency takes on more responsibility for further aspects of the work. All leaders throughout the Agency are involved in a variety of ways with their stakeholders. To enhance the way we understand and respond to customer needs Agency Quality Council reviewed and evaluated the way customer complaints were dealt with. As a result a plan of action was developed to ensure the process improved. Stakeholders are rewarded for their involvement by using their feedback to inform the development of Policy and Strategy.

We are a member of the Centre for Competitiveness and have assigned a resource to help work as an assessor on site visits for the "Steps" award.

We measure our performance with others to learn and improve the way we do things. To help us do this we attend external seminars and develop external partnerships.

SMALL/MEDIUM

Our philosophy that all six of us are "leaders" and cover each other's responsibilities does mean that there is little difference between what the company does and what its leaders do. A larger company might have a sales-force to whom leaders could role model actions and behaviours symbolic of customer and partner empathy. For us, this is not the case. There is no one, other than leaders, who might be involved externally and so this is an overview of such involvement.

In our early years, we did adopt a rather scattergun-approach to customer contact i.e. we saw as many customers as possible and put a lot of effort into reacting to their requests and dealing with their problems. Over time, this way of working has evolved into a structured approach of managing customer relationships, anticipating their needs and preventing problems arising.

We believe most strongly that success in managing customer relationships is critical to our overall success. It is enshrined in our Mission that we will become the most successful sales company within the Group by developing even closer relationships with our customers and suppliers and one of our values is to exceed customers' needs by anticipation and planning.

We are proud of how we operate and take pride in showing off our business to customers and suppliers. As a result, we encourage key partners to visit us, so they can get a better feel for how we do things. This approach also enables office-based staff to put a face to a name. Every member of our staff will meet a customer face to face at least once a month and more frequently according to their main area of responsibility.

Links to Fundamental Concepts

☑ Leadership and constancy of purpose
☐ Management by process and facts
☐ People development and involvement
☐ Continuous learning, improvement and innovation
☑ Customer focus
☑ Partner development
☐ Public responsibility
☑ Results orientation

Links to Fundamental Concepts

☑ Leadership and constancy of purpose
☐ Management by process and facts
☐ People development and involvement
☐ Continuous learning, improvement and innovation
☑ Customer focus
☑ Partner development
☐ Public responsibility
☐ Results orientation

Criterion 1

3.1 | Leadership

How leaders develop and facilitate the achievement of the mission and vision, develop values required for long-term success and implement these via appropriate actions and behaviours, and are personally involved in ensuring the organisation's management system is developed and implemented.

Sub-criterion 1D:
Leaders motivate, support and recognise the organisation's people.

Areas to address may include:

- *Personally communicating the organisation's mission, vision, values, policy and strategy, plans objectives and targets to people;*

- *Being accessible, actively listening and responding to people;*

- *Helping and supporting people to achieve their plans, objectives and targets;*

- *Encouraging and enabling people to participate in improvement activity;*

- *Recognising both team and individual efforts, at all levels within the organisation, in a timely and appropriate manner.*

PRIVATE SECTOR

Key events at which the Company's entire Executive Management Team communicates Vision and Values and Strategic Direction are the yearly all-employee forums, twice-yearly manager briefings and three monthly employee forums. Other leaders supplement these channels with ongoing daily communications. In addition, a wide range of Senior Managers participate in employee induction programme presenting the Company's Vision, Strategy and Targets to new starters.

Following review, measurement of the deployment of Vision and Values was introduced. Results show the effectiveness of the approaches in achieving wide deployment and driving the creation of a single company culture: All of the approaches indicated above in support of communicating Vision, Values and Strategy have associated direct question and answer activities.

The employee forum process has a particular role to play in providing access to leaders as this happens on a more frequent basis and allows a greater amount of discussion, leading to direct leadership action.

Following feedback and a review of its approaches the Executive Management Team has implemented a site visit programme to increase their personal accessibility and allow employees to meet directors and discuss issues of concern.

The Executive Management Team and Development Steering Group review process performance during the year and annually review and improve the approaches for helping people to achieve objectives and targets.

Links to Fundamental Concepts

☑ Leadership and constancy of purpose	☐ Customer focus
	☐ Partner development
☐ Management by process and facts	☐ Public responsibility
	☐ Results orientation
☐ People development and involvement	
☐ Continuous learning, improvement and innovation	

Criterion 1

PUBLIC SECTOR

The Staffing Committee meets at least twice a term to review and discuss issues relating to the organisation's personnel.

The key issue throughout the year was the recruitment and retention of staff, particularly teaching staff. The School was fortunate to end the year (and start the current academic year) with a full complement of staff, despite a difficult year for all schools in the area owing to general teacher shortages.

Together with other committees of the Governing Body, the Staffing Committee spent considerable time during the year reviewing its policies and putting in place a comprehensive and up-to-date set of policies for the School in order to assist the staff deliver effective teaching. The Head Teacher and Department Heads communicate these to staff. Staff are encouraged to participate in extra curricular activities. We are very appreciative of the amount of hard work, personal time and dedication of staff that organise these activities which is communicated to those individuals involved and acknowledged through their peer group.

Other issues discussed included the implementation of Performance Management, introduction (eventually) of Threshold Reviews for teachers, and the appraisal of non-teaching staff.

Attention is paid to measures that might be introduced to monitor/improve staff morale and the Committee held a number of discussions on the distressing outbreak of damage to teachers' property outside the School in the latter part of the year. A behaviour programme is in place to change pupils' behaviour patterns to the good. Staff play an active role in this programme with their pupils which is not only for the benefit of the pupils but also has a positive affect on staff morale, the teachers teach and the pupils learn.

SMALL/MEDIUM

Six monthly review of progress with all employees on a one to one basis has been introduced. Each manager attends a quarterly review with the General Manager to ensure all personal and departmental/factory goals and objectives are being maintained. The manager then takes up issues with his departmental/factory and direct reports.

A further improvement in the appraisal system is the introduction of a 360-degree performance appraisal for senior managers. The General Manager and European Controller participate in this process. Succession planning is undertaken to help ensure a secure future. The policy is to promote internally whenever possible. One of the key aspects in selection is the employee's record of supporting improvement initiatives. The general manager keeps the records and discusses them at the quarterly reviews with the managers. All employees are actively encouraged to support and participate in improvement activities. In fact the culture is to promote learning through participation.

Every year since 1994 100% of our employees have participated on at least one improvement team. This year the goal is to have 95% of all employees participating in at least two improvement activities. This measure is part of the Quality Improvement Team responsibility and is reviewed as a Quality Operating System measure.

Quality Leaders have the job of encouraging employees to submit improvement ideas through the (Involvement) programme. In the past we won the award for achieving the best results in (Participation by Everyone), of the whole of the Corporation. Every year all employees attend a half-day meeting off site where the best team projects are presented.

Links to Fundamental Concepts

☑ Leadership and constancy of purpose

☐ Management by process and facts

☐ People development and involvement

☐ Continuous learning, improvement and innovation

☑ Customer focus

☐ Partner development

☐ Public responsibility

☐ Results orientation

Links to Fundamental Concepts

☑ Leadership and constancy of purpose

☐ Management by process and facts

☑ People development and involvement

☑ Continuous learning, improvement and innovation

☐ Customer focus

☐ Partner development

☐ Public responsibility

☐ Results orientation

Criterion 1

The Excellence Model

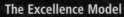

Enablers   **Results**

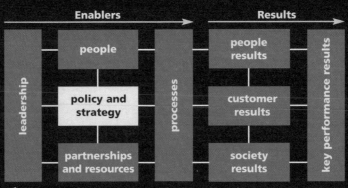

leadership	people		processes	people results	key performance results
	policy and strategy			customer results	
	partnerships and resources			society results	

Innovation and Learning

© *1999 EFQM.*

"Leaders develop a policy and strategy based on the organisation's capabilities and on stakeholders' needs, and ensure it is reviewed, updated, communicated and implemented."

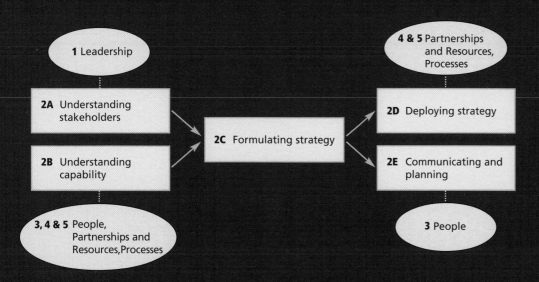

1 Leadership

4 & 5 Partnerships and Resources, Processes

2A Understanding stakeholders

2B Understanding capability

2C Formulating strategy

2D Deploying strategy

2E Communicating and planning

3, 4 & 5 People, Partnerships and Resources, Processes

3 People

Linkages between the sub-criteria and with the other enablers

3.2 | Policy and Strategy

How the organisation implements its mission and vision via a clear stakeholder-focused strategy, supported by relevant policies, plans, objectives, targets and processes.

Sub-criterion 2A:

Policy and strategy are based on the present and future needs and expectations of stakeholders.

Areas to address may include:

- *Gathering and understanding information to define the market and market segment the organisation will operate in both now and in the future;*

- *Understanding and anticipating the needs and expectations of customers, employees, partners, society and shareholders, as appropriate;*

- *Understanding and anticipating developments in the market place, including competitor activity.*

PRIVATE SECTOR

A detailed review of the needs of the major stakeholders, competitors, market and industry conditions led to the establishment of some focussed top-level goals for the organization. These goals, which were set for a 1999–2004 timeframe, centred on growth in both revenue and profitability.

To communicate the stakeholder needs to business areas, these needs were translated into a programme, which is termed 'Path to Growth'. Path to Growth goes beyond the basic financial targets to embrace a set of strategic thrusts that provide guidance on how the long-term goals will be achieved. A business graphic or logo has been designed detailing these thrusts, which includes 'hard' deliverables such as supply chain performance as well as 'softer' elements such as the enabling culture that is desired. These areas support the needs of other stakeholders, such as employees and the community. Each area of the programme has a set of clear performance objectives.

A unique feature of the approach is the communication strategy to support consistency of purpose, where many communication channels have been activated. A summary brochure containing an outline of the programme and the targets has been produced and issued to all staff. The communication is supported by other vehicles such as the use of the programme logo as a computer screensaver. The logo and details of programme appear regularly in company magazines, both at the corporate and business group level.

The programme appears regularly on company presentations and web pages. As an example, the chairman's web page has a link to a 'Path to Growth' area that details progress to date and success stories. This focus of the programme is maintained at all leadership levels of the organisation.

The consistent reinforcement of the message through the communication channels has also enabled the re-focusing of the message as the programme has evolved. Following the first year of the programme significant progress was made in a number of areas. Following a review, at the start of the second year, the main messages were repeated and progress communicated. It was also decided to focus the activity onto three primary areas in order to create 'a space for growth'.

Links to Fundamental Concepts

☑ Leadership and constancy of purpose	☐ Customer focus
	☐ Partner development
☑ Management by process and facts	☐ Public responsibility
☐ People development and involvement	☑ Results orientation
☐ Continuous learning, improvement and innovation	

Criterion 2

PUBLIC SECTOR

Our mission statement, "Working together to provide Best Value services", has been developed to display our commitment to partnerships with all of our stakeholders.

The focus of our business planning process is the annual strategic workshop to which inputs regarding our stakeholders are brought.

Operational Services is a significant part of the County Council, which comprises 66 councillors, or members, elected to office on a four yearly cycle. The members have developed 5 Strategic Statements providing direction for the County Council. They are reviewed and updated annually.

More detail regarding objectives is provided and a Local Performance Plan is developed and issued to residents each year. Below that a Corporate Business Plan provides targets for officers to work to. A working group developed the first last year. It was led by our Director in order to benefit from our experience. Having established the approach, the current plan has been developed through a series of workshops; one for each Strategic Statement. Representatives from our Directorate Management Team participated with other officers and members to each workshop.

Included within the 66 councillors are 13 appointed to Operational Services Committee to oversee our activities. They are responsible for guiding and approving our policy and strategy and monitoring our performance.

The needs and expectations of society are gathered and expressed by members. In addition to their daily contact with the public, perception is also gathered through a mobile information unit, a street survey, a questionnaire attached to the Local Performance Plan, a district joint survey and focus groups and a citizen's panel of 1000 residents set up by MORI.

SMALL/MEDIUM

The College is now at a critical stage publicly proving the sustainability of the principle of beacon schools to pioneer the very best practice. After 10 or so years, the College has the confidence and expertise to lead into the next stage of national education development. Our development plan recognises the importance we attach to the needs of all stakeholders, and the planning process is the subject of regular review and refinement.

The next five years are potentially most exciting but also very challenging times for the College. Visitors tell us that what we have achieved to date is incredible. We believe that we have met with a high degree of success when using indicators such as assessment and examination results, OFSTED inspection reports, attendance levels, business and community involvement and the light in the students' eyes as they go about their work. However, the College intends to sustain its developments at the cutting edge of educational innovations and improvements for students' learning.

Following careful evaluation of the overall approach of the College within the Governors and senior management review process the College is about to make the next step. This is the development of the Academy and Federation, which will disseminate College's expertise nationally. The emphasis will be in 3 broad themes:
- Continue to improve standards and add value.
- Continue to improve the quality of learning provision for 21st Century Citizenship.
- Further the programme of linking with the Community and other Schools so as to share the College's expertise on advanced practices and facilities made possible by its status and staff commitment and thereby add to cost effectiveness, national improvement and international reputation.

Links to Fundamental Concepts

☑ Leadership and constancy of purpose

☐ Management by process and facts

☐ People development and involvement

☑ Continuous learning, improvement and innovation

☑ Customer focus

☐ Partner development

☑ Public responsibility

☑ Results orientation

Links to Fundamental Concepts

☑ Leadership and constancy of purpose

☐ Management by process and facts

☐ People development and involvement

☑ Continuous learning, improvement and innovation

☑ Customer focus

☐ Partner development

☐ Public responsibility

☑ Results orientation

Criterion 2

3.2 | Policy and Strategy

How the organisation implements its mission and vision via a clear stakeholder-focused strategy, supported by relevant policies, plans, objectives, targets and processes.

Sub-criterion 2B:
Policy and strategy are based on information from performance measures, research, learning and creativity related activities.

Areas to address may include:

- *Collecting and understanding output from internal performance indicators;*

- *Collecting and understanding the output from learning activities;*

- *Analysing the performance of competitors and best in class organisations;*

- *Understanding social, environmental and legal issues;*

- *Identifying and understanding economic and demographic indicators;*

- *Understanding the impact of new technologies;*

- *Analysing and using stakeholders' ideas.*

PRIVATE SECTOR

Internal data is sourced via our own performance monitoring records, enabling us to identify process improvement priorities. Upward information is also sought from our employees, via our employee survey. Input-output analysis, capacity planning and process capability studies are undertaken during our (Departmental business and technical analysis) process.

The importance placed on the data sources during the policy development process reflects the over-riding business situation and needs of the time. The last 12 months have been directed strongly on 'profitability and competitiveness', which is reflected in our emphasis on increasing value-added productivity. Following our annual policy review for 1999 the revised goal was significantly more difficult with a 'breakthrough' approach required to redefine our cost base and increase competitiveness.

The recent policy review for 2000 the then Senior Management Team that included the Manufacturing Director and Finance Manager concluded 'customer perceived value', is to be the next step in building our company's competitive edge.

Due to the extremely competitive nature of the market-place direct competitor analysis is not available, although competitor analysis is carried out for us as an operational unit by the Europe Sales Divisions. The organisation gains other contributory benchmark performance data through involvement in several activities: Supply chain and materials benchmarking is through involvement with the annual KPMG Supply Chain Excellence Awards. In 1999 we were winners of the 'Most improved company' category, in 2000 we were one of six finalists.

Links to Fundamental Concepts

☑ Leadership and constancy of purpose	☐ Customer focus
	☐ Partner development
☑ Management by process and facts	☐ Public responsibility
☐ People development and involvement	☐ Results orientation
☑ Continuous learning, improvement and innovation	

PUBLIC SECTOR

The Agency has linked its programme of Better Quality Service reviews (part of the Modernising Government Initiative to improve service within the public sector) to the European Foundation for Quality Management Excellence Model. Self-assessment is conducted of the function or service subject to a Better Quality Service review. The assessment provides a benchmark from which to conduct the Better Quality Service review and helps the review process to concentrate on areas for improvement identified during the self-assessment.

Better Quality Service reviews lead to change in the delivery of services. The impact of this change can be evaluated objectively by conducting a further self-assessment once the recommendations from a Better Quality Service review have been implemented. Our experience has shown that self-assessments and Better Quality Service reviews usually identify similar problems. This helps to reinforce the need to change as staff identified the issues themselves.

SMALL/MEDIUM

The College Development Plan sets targets with performance indicators that are agreed with teams.

Primarily, the plan incorporates educational needs, both as decreed by the Government and the Department for Education and Employment, and those required by students, parents, the community, industry and society. To enable this, relevant and comprehensible information is obtained from 3 areas:
- performance measurement
- discussion and research with institutions and learned bodies
- learning and creativity activity.

We continually benchmark both internally against 'best in class'. Internally, this will include subject results at each key stage, and resources and budgets used to achieve these targets. We also use feedback from the customers – students and staff – themselves. Curriculum material is innovated and levels of achievement and ideas generated in all areas are used as parameters to produce consistently good outcomes.

Externally, we review competitors and partners to understand their mission, aims and objectives, strategies and technological strengths and weaknesses. Statistical analyses based on examination results from our competitor organisations such as local schools, national schools are carried out. The College does, however, go beyond simply benchmarking educational establishments. It also uses the 'best in class' from business, industry and public services, to the extent that benefits accrued from performance measurement and benchmarking have been recognised by the awards won and interest shown by other establishments.

Links to Fundamental Concepts

☐ Leadership and constancy of purpose

☑ Management by process and facts

☐ People development and involvement

☐ Continuous learning, improvement and innovation

☐ Customer focus

☐ Partner development

☐ Public responsibility

☐ Results orientation

Links to Fundamental Concepts

☑ Leadership and constancy of purpose

☑ Management by process and facts

☐ People development and involvement

☑ Continuous learning, improvement and innovation

☑ Customer focus

☐ Partner development

☑ Public responsibility

☐ Results orientation

Criterion 2

3.2 | Policy and Strategy

How the organisation implements its mission and vision via a clear stakeholder-focused strategy, supported by relevant policies, plans, objectives, targets and processes.

Sub-criterion 2C:
Policy and strategy are developed, reviewed and updated.

Areas to address may include:

- *Developing policy and strategy consistent with the organisation's mission, vision and values and based on the needs and expectations of stakeholders and information from learning and innovation activities;*

- *Balancing the needs and expectations of stakeholders;*

- *Balancing short and long-term pressures and requirements;*

- *Developing alternative scenarios and contingency plans to address risks;*

- *Identifying present and future competitive advantage;*

- *Aligning the organisation's policy and strategy with that of partners;*

- *Reflecting the fundamental concepts of Excellence in policy and strategy;*

- *Evaluating the relevance and effectiveness of policy and strategy;*

- *Identifying critical success factors;*

- *Reviewing and updating policy and strategy.*

PRIVATE SECTOR

Our planning process provides the framework for defining our strategies and policies, generating business objectives and translating them into Corporate and Business Unit Balanced Scorecard key performance targets. Individual objectives and targets, which support these plans and scorecards, are then drawn up. Our strategic planning process is a top down framework that provides all our managers with a set of top-down guideline strategies that link and harmonise all our company wide objectives, targets, scorecards and improvement initiatives.

The use of the Excellence Model has helped us refocus our overall approach to delivering the principles of continuous and breakthrough improvements through our strategy and policies. We use the Excellence Model as a tool to help measure the effectiveness of our strategies against our results. In order to ensure the deployment of improvement activities across all our businesses, our managers are assigned as action-owners of areas from improvement identified from our annual assessments against the Model. We brief updates on our scorecard performance monthly.

During the past five years we have further developed our strategy and policies to reflect the changing needs of our stakeholders. Our scorecards help us to ensure that we attempt to balance the needs and expectations of all four sections of the scorecard i.e. in providing customer service excellence, maximising shareholder value, improving internal processes and developing growth and innovation.

Our Executive team maintains our rolling 3-year plan on an annual cycle, using a top-down planning methodology with bottom up input through feedback from our people. Our annual planning schedule covers around 4 months, with the production of a series of iterative drafts of the following year's plan and budgets based on scenario planning and end-of-year performance estimates.

Links to Fundamental Concepts

☑ Leadership and constancy of purpose	☐ Customer focus
☑ Management by process and facts	☐ Partner development
☐ People development and involvement	☐ Public responsibility
☐ Continuous learning, improvement and innovation	☑ Results orientation

PUBLIC SECTOR The content of the office business plan is debated at our staff conference where delegates consider what is required during the next 12 months. Delegates comprise the senior management team together with representatives from the staff and the local trade union.

Agency policy requirements, key performance targets, customer and staff survey results and issues arising from self-assessment and IiP are all considered when formulating the Plan. Publication of a single sheet business plan then follows conference. This is split into three sections: (a) our commitment and objective, (b) a record of office performance against our key performance targets and (c) specific action points relating to the implementation and development of projects arising from debate at conference.

The Business Plan is supplemented by an additional document, which details each of the action points against their specific criterion within the Excellence Model. An owner is identified for each action who ensures that the action is completed within set targets. They will also monitor the results achieved and review the outcome. The action owner, target dates and method of review are all incorporated in the supplemental document to the business plan.

Progress against the Business Plan and supplemental document is reviewed at monthly meetings of the Senior Management Team. At these meetings each Criterion Owner will provide reports based on the findings from the projects/action points. The Team considers recommendations based on these findings and their conclusions incorporated into the Business Plan and Supplemental Document. Both the Plan and Document are published on the local Intranet so that all staff have the opportunity to see the goals for the office and how we are progressing month on month.

SMALL/MEDIUM Strategies and policies for the business are developed each year when the current business plan is updated at the annual strategic review. An appropriate set of strategic objectives for the future direction of the company is decided by the Executive Team/Management Team. These take into account how the team would like the organisation to grow in the next 3-year period. For the past 4 years the key objectives of the company have remained unchanged as they are entirely appropriate for maintaining consistency with the vision and mission of the organisation, all of them being based on continuous improvement and the expectations of stakeholders.

The strategies for obtaining these objectives change as improved processes, management techniques, training and new technologies develop and as priorities change. The Executive Team/Management Team discuss any new or revised policies or strategies that need to be introduced to our processes in order to meet the key objectives. Targets are set for projected sales to each market which leads to new targets for marketing, capital equipment, employment levels, training and Management Information Systems to keep up with the growth in production.

The needs and expectations of all stakeholders are reviewed on a regular basis. It is important to keep everyone happy and this involves having a balanced approach and ensuring that satisfying one stakeholder will not be to the detriment of another. Improvements to one stakeholder can have a positive knock on effect on all other stakeholders, e.g. improvements to our supply of raw material has benefited our customers, employees, suppliers and ultimately, our shareholders and the local community.

Two years ago at the Strategic Review, turnover figures were set and these have just been revised. Each time the turnover targets are revised, the number of machines and employee levels are also reviewed and revised to keep abreast of the production increases required.

Links to Fundamental Concepts

- ☑ Leadership and constancy of purpose
- ☑ Management by process and facts
- ☐ People development and involvement
- ☐ Continuous learning, improvement and innovation
- ☐ Customer focus
- ☐ Partner development
- ☐ Public responsibility
- ☑ Results orientation

Links to Fundamental Concepts

- ☑ Leadership and constancy of purpose
- ☐ Management by process and facts
- ☐ People development and involvement
- ☐ Continuous learning, improvement and innovation
- ☐ Customer focus
- ☐ Partner development
- ☐ Public responsibility
- ☑ Results orientation

3.2 | Policy and Strategy

How the organisation implements its mission and vision via a clear stakeholder-focused strategy, supported by relevant policies, plans, objectives, targets and processes.

Sub-criterion 2D:
Policy and strategy are deployed through a framework of key processes.

Areas to address may include:

- *Identifying and designing the framework of key processes needed to deliver the organisation's policy and strategy;*

- *Establishing clear ownership of the key processes;*

- *Defining the key processes including the identification of stakeholders;*

- *Reviewing the effectiveness of the framework of key processes to deliver policy and strategy.*

PRIVATE SECTOR

The Company's methodology for identifying and managing key strategic programmes in a systematic manner is a tremendous asset. This, coupled with the dedication and team spirit that pervades the organisation, makes it a very successful unit.

The Company has an integrated planning and operational management system. Overall strategy is reviewed quarterly by the Board, with periodic (normally annual) externally-facilitated strategy workshops. Key processes and process owners are identified or reviewed and effective measures on how to ensure that key processes are delivering to plan are agreed.

Programmes and projects that are classified as critical to delivering strategic objectives are identified in the Annual Quality Plan and Budget, and are reviewed monthly by the Board. Process ownership is allocated to functional managers who are best placed to deliver process goals and objectives through their functional management and communication processes. Top-level measures are included in the Company Balanced Scorecard.

In addition to its role in linking strategy and operational plans, the Scorecard is published on the Intranet as a communications tool. Strategy Focus Workshops, available to anyone in the Company with an interest in the basics of strategic management and how it is applied, are an additional channel for strategy communication. The development of a Balanced Scorecard is one of the syndicate exercises used in these workshops.

Links to Fundamental Concepts

- ☑ Leadership and constancy of purpose
- ☐ Customer focus
- ☑ Management by process and facts
- ☐ Partner development
- ☐ Public responsibility
- ☐ People development and involvement
- ☑ Results orientation
- ☐ Continuous learning, improvement and innovation

PUBLIC SECTOR

Policy and strategy are deployed via the following key processes:

Service Planning – the development of the department's Service Plan, including the determination and allocation of resources is undertaken annually through a formal planning process, taking account of County Council and customer priorities.

Service Delivery – implementation of the agreed Service Plan with regular monitoring and review.

Service Review – formal review of the Service Plan that feeds back into service planning.

Clear ownership of key processes is defined in the Department's Service Plan and in individual Job Descriptions, which define areas of responsibility and provide clear lines of management/direction.

As indicated above, Policy and Strategy are deployed via the following cycle of key processes:

Service Planning – The service planning process led by the Departmental Management Team involves the translation of corporate objectives, policies and strategies into an annual Departmental Service Plan which identifies: departmental objectives and key tasks, section key tasks, departmental strategic training and development plan, personal action and training/development plans, resources required to deliver the plan. The County Council's property portfolio determines the responsibility for each property and this in turn helps to establish the nature and extent of services to be provided to particular clients or client groups.

Service Delivery – departmental, Section, Personal Action Plans and agreed work programmes form the basis for the delivery of services by the department's three business units. Progress is monitored regularly throughout the year via various different meeting forums involving staff, managers, suppliers and clients.

Review – review of deployment is achieved through regular monthly review at DMT of progress against the Service Plan. There are special DMT meetings twice yearly at which the overall deployment of the department's policy and strategy is reviewed.

Links to Fundamental Concepts

☑ Leadership and constancy of purpose
☑ Customer focus
☑ Management by process and facts
☐ Partner development
☐ Public responsibility
☐ Results orientation
☑ People development and involvement
☐ Continuous learning, improvement and innovation

SMALL/MEDIUM

Our Managing Director developed the first framework of Key Processes when we moved to our new premises in 1994. These were based on the Group framework first used in 1986–7 as part of its Quality in Physical Distribution. Since then we have gradually migrated from the Quality in Physical Distribution format initially to accommodate BS5750, followed by ISO9002. The framework has been continuously refined to the extent that there are now 24 Key Processes, of which 11 are deemed to be Critical Key Processes. This process framework is the cornerstone and drives the agenda which is also used to indicate when the next process is due for review and who will lead the discussion.

Every member of staff is an owner of certain processes. Responsibilities of a Process Owner are clearly defined.

At the end of every year, we review whether the ownership of key processes is still relevant or process ownership rotation might be beneficial. If responsibilities or the process itself have changed during the year, or perhaps someone's experience or expertise has developed, a change of ownership may be agreed. If so, job descriptions and Personal Development Folders would be revised to reflect the changes.

All Key Processes are defined and documented by means of the agenda, which also identifies interested stakeholders. In recent years, we have vastly improved our knowledge of process variation and capability, following visits to other companies and attendance at courses on Statistical Process control.

Because the Key Processes, and their performance are so fundamentally important to the achievement of our policy and strategy, we subject them to regular review. However, as well as reviewing process performance, we also regularly take high level view of the totality of the process framework and the approaches we employ in using the process framework to achieve our policy and strategy. The entire framework of key processes is formally reviewed annually at the year-end and is tested against the delivery of our Business Objectives.

Links to Fundamental Concepts

☑ Leadership and constancy of purpose
☐ Customer focus
☑ Management by process and facts
☐ Partner development
☐ Public responsibility
☑ Results orientation
☐ People development and involvement
☐ Continuous learning, improvement and innovation

Criterion 2

3.2 Policy and Strategy

How the organisation implements its mission and vision via a clear stakeholder-focused strategy, supported by relevant policies, plans, objectives, targets and processes.

Sub-criterion 2E:
Policy and strategy are communicated and implemented.

Areas to address may include:

- *Communicating and cascading policy and strategy, as appropriate;*

- *Using policy and strategy as the basis for planning activities and the setting of objectives and targets throughout the organisation;*

- *Aligning, prioritising, agreeing and communicating plans, objectives and targets;*

- *Evaluating the awareness of policy and strategy.*

PRIVATE SECTOR

Our Strategic planning and policy deployment process is based on the Japanese concept of *hosin kanri*, which simply means 'management of pointing the way'. The Strategic plan and policy are deployed through the organisation via Departmental Policy Plans and into individual objectives at manager, supervisor and engineer levels. Our 5-point plan process supports this deployment as a means of identifying cost reduction or value adding opportunities.

These opportunities are translated into specific objectives with identified responsibilities, which are then deployed as individual objectives at engineer and manager level, with supporting 'sub-objectives' deployed at supervisor and team leader level. Progress review of these objectives is undertaken weekly accumulating achievements upwards from sub-objectives to objectives to company goal. The process is closely aligned and supported by the Department planning processes, to facilitate the achievement of investment and operational plans.

The organisation has a well structured communication framework which facilitates an effective flow of information up, down and across the organisation and includes external communication to customers, suppliers and to sister organisations who support our manufacturing processes through their sales or support processes. Key communication vehicles include: team briefing for periodic cascades, supervisory briefings by the Manufacturing Director and his team together with consultative forums and team meetings.

All Departments display policy, targets and progress within the workplace. The Human Resource Leader, who determine the media, timings and company content as part of the total planning process, undertakes all planning for the communication of policy and strategy. The Manufacturing Director and his team give initial policy briefings to all employees as one of the quarterly senior team presentations to employees.

Links to Fundamental Concepts

☑ Leadership and constancy of purpose

☑ Management by process and facts

☐ People development and involvement

☐ Continuous learning, improvement and innovation

☐ Customer focus

☐ Partner development

☐ Public responsibility

☐ Results orientation

Criterion 2

PUBLIC SECTOR

The implementation of Lotus Notes in 1997 provided a valuable mechanism to enable information relating to policy and strategy to be communicated throughout the Department. It was a key strategic decision to provide access to Lotus Notes to all office-based members of staff, and in 2000 this was extended to include all members of staff by providing access to field-based workers.

Examples of information communicated via Lotus Notes:
- the Departmental Service Plan (part of the Service Management System)
- Team Briefing notes
- Meetings Database (Agendas and Minutes of all Departmental Meetings)
- E-mail
- Corporate Bulletin Board (business and social)
- Quality Management System (Quality Assurance Manual and Quality Assurance Audit programme)
- the Health and Safety Manual
- Committee Reports
- Project Management System
- lists of Contractors and Consultants and Croner's Premises Management publication Document Libraries (corporate and departmental)
- Property Asset Register/File List
- Corporate Consultation Database.

The Departmental Service Plan is formally presented to all staff each year, providing an opportunity for discussion in relation to all aspects of our business. This year's event was held in the Council Chamber in and involved a presentation by the Director of Property Services and a Councillor reviewing last year's performance and confirming the key objectives for the next year.

Other sessions are held to communicate key initiatives as they happen, for example in 1998 the Chief Executive and Director of Property Services gave a presentation to all staff on the Best Value initiative, and previously there have been presentations on the implementation of Quality Assurance and the effects of Compulsory Competitive Tendering.

Links to Fundamental Concepts

- ☑ Leadership and constancy of purpose
- ☑ Management by process and facts
- ☐ People development and involvement
- ☐ Continuous learning, improvement and innovation
- ☐ Customer focus
- ☐ Partner development
- ☐ Public responsibility
- ☐ Results orientation

SMALL/MEDIUM

Whilst there is a 5 year Plan in place detailing where the business needs to be/wants to be, the Company utilises a Quality Steering team which meets monthly to detail and review key critical plans and monitor performance. The Company utilise a Road Map based around the European Foundation for Quality Management Excellence Model, to ensure that all aspects are covered and planned for, thus the Company maintains an impetus of continuous improvement.

The road map contains all key processes and projects required to meet the Company's objectives, with responsibilities, times and dates for completion. The utilisation of the Road Map allows the Board to instigate and monitor teams that may work on continuous improvement, problem solving and corrective action teams. All aspects of the crux of the model are utilised throughout the Company to ensure that the Company understands and utilises the key enablers driving them towards a successful Results, all aspects of the model are passed to everyone within the facility.

Having processes that support and drive the Enablers of the EFQM Excellence Model gives us the confidence that we have the ability to communicate our policy and strategy through all aspects of our Company.

Links to Fundamental Concepts

- ☑ Leadership and constancy of purpose
- ☑ Management by process and facts
- ☐ People development and involvement
- ☑ Continuous learning, improvement and innovation
- ☑ Customer focus
- ☐ Partner development
- ☐ Public responsibility
- ☐ Results orientation

Criterion 2

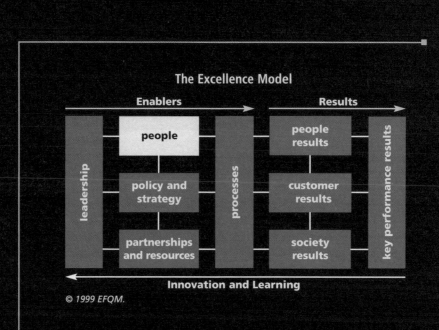

The Excellence Model

Enablers

Results

leadership

people

policy and
strategy

partnerships
and resources

processes

people
results

customer
results

society
results

key performance results

Innovation and Learning

© 1999 EFQM.

"Leaders ensure the organisation has the necessary quality and quantity of staff, and that they are cared for, listened to and recognised, to deliver its policy and strategy."

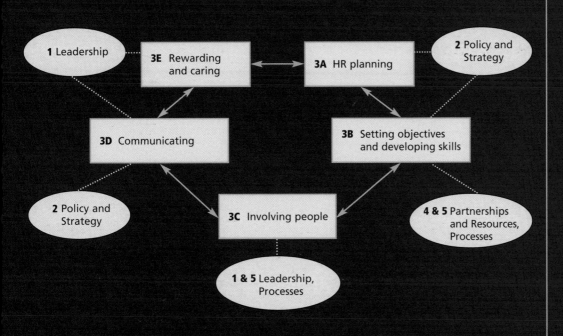

1 Leadership

3E Rewarding and caring

3A HR planning

2 Policy and Strategy

3D Communicating

3B Setting objectives and developing skills

2 Policy and Strategy

3C Involving people

4 & 5 Partnerships and Resources, Processes

1 & 5 Leadership, Processes

Linkages between the sub-criteria and with the other enablers

3.3 | People

ow the organisation manages, develops and releases the knowledge and full potential of its people at an individual, team-based and organisation-wide level, and plans these activities in order to support its policy and strategy and the effective operation of its processes.

Sub-criterion 3A:

People resources are planned, managed and improved.

Areas to address may include:

- *Developing human resource policies, strategies and plans;*

- *Involving employees, and their representatives, in developing human resource policies, strategies and plans;*

- *Aligning the human resource plans with policy and strategy, the organisational structure and the framework of key processes;*

- *Managing recruitment and career development;*

- *Ensuring fairness in all terms of employment, including equal opportunities;*

- *Using people surveys and other forms of employee feedback to improve human resource policies, strategies and plans;*

- *Using innovative organisation methodologies to improve ways of working, e.g. restructuring the supply chain, matrix working, flexible team working, high performance work teams.*

PRIVATE SECTOR

Our people are the main source of our overall flexibility and people management is recognised as one of our business critical processes. In the early 90s customer audits and competency expectations began to emphasise the link between the business planning and people development processes, in addition to the direct manufacturing capability provided by ISO9000. We realised that, like ISO9000, Investors in People (IiP) would become a key standard for suppliers in our industrial sector. As a result of this, during the business planning process of 1992, the Management Team agreed to a policy direction that would achieve IiP certification. This objective was achieved in September 1993, and we were successfully re-certified in 1996, 1999 and 2001.

Our achievement of ISO9000 and 'Investors' enabled us to move rapidly to QS9000 certification in 1997. IiP was also an underpinning aspect of our achieving the ISO14001 environmental standard certification in November 1998.

During the general recession in manufacturing in 1993 the organisation recognised that radical changes were required within its operating structure in order to remain competitive in the rapidly fluctuating economic climate. At its annual planning workshop in 1994 the Senior Management Team developed the Business Transformation approach. This provided the basis for aligning our Human Resource strategy with the policy and process review and change management from 1994 to 2000, covering two of our Challenge periods 1994–1996 and 2000.

The Business Transformation plan has driven the introduction of many changes and developments in working methodology, aimed at increasing our capability for adaptability, flexibility and responsiveness. These capabilities are essential in meeting the increasing demands of our customers and the marketplace in which we compete.

Links to Fundamental Concepts

☑ Leadership and constancy of purpose

☐ Management by process and facts

☑ People development and involvement

☑ Continuous learning, improvement and innovation

☐ Customer focus

☐ Partner development

☐ Public responsibility

☐ Results orientation

Criterion 3

PUBLIC SECTOR

We develop our People Strategy in the context of the Values, national priorities and a range of inputs, for example integrated consultation with all District and Regional Teams, with improvement groups and with Trade Union representatives. The Regional HR Manager presents a draft strategy at our Annual Planning conference. It sets our approach to HR issues and promotes our people priorities so that each team is equipped to agree actions under the "People" Value in their Business Delivery Plan.

The strategy addresses the HR implications of any changes in Annual Performance Agreement priorities and resource for the year ahead. The strategy is finalised at the conference. We measure the effectiveness of our strategy formulation process through Excellence assessment and in response; have involved Regional Business Team members at an earlier stage in the process year on year. The effectiveness of our People Strategy throughout the year is reviewed through bi-lateral meetings of the HR Manager with each Regional Business Team member and through feedback received at the monthly Regional Business Team meeting.

In developing our People Strategy for 2000/01 additional consultation on region wide actions related to Leadership and People was carried out with the Regional Business Team, through a one day event prior to the Planning Conference. The Regional Business Team reviewed evidence from our Regional People survey, from assessment against the Equality Framework and from the review of Leadership completed by all managers at our Annual Business Conference, together with our approach to the collection and use of people data.

We use a competence framework as the basis for vacancy filling and recruitment. The process involves specifying the competencies and behavioural indicators required for each job. All internal and external applicants for vacancies provide evidence to match the specified competencies from their working experience. All vacancies are open to full or part-time applicants. Around one in four of our people work part-time.

SMALL/MEDIUM

Our Company conducts a comprehensive appraisal system for all staff twice a year. Performance is measured against an expectation skill set for each position, providing staff with visibility of the requirements to achieve promotion.

The personal development plan integrates the business objectives with personal objectives and identifies any training needs. This information is used to develop the training budget for the year ahead. Software systems capture feedback from delegates and track the success of particular courses.

The company combines traditional in-house and external training with the following innovative training techniques to develop its staff, e.g.
- a comprehensive monthly induction programme for new employees
- Professional Studies supported by the company through study leave days and funding for courses and exam fees
- the Company University which is conducted on a regular basis by staff and for staff to harness individual skills, knowledge and experience to further develop the skills of other staff
- Mentoring Scheme to encourage employees to gain career guidance and support from a colleague
- Graduate Training Scheme accredited by the Institute of Electrical Engineers
- team-building events held twice a year for all staff to undertake a wide range of activities to learn valuable skills that can be applied to their jobs.

Links to Fundamental Concepts

☐ Leadership and constancy of purpose
☐ Management by process and facts
☑ People development and involvement
☐ Continuous learning, improvement and innovation
☐ Customer focus
☐ Partner development
☐ Public responsibility
☐ Results orientation

Links to Fundamental Concepts

☑ Leadership and constancy of purpose
☐ Management by process and facts
☑ People development and involvement
☐ Continuous learning, improvement and innovation
☐ Customer focus
☐ Partner development
☐ Public responsibility
☐ Results orientation

Criterion 3

3.3 | People

How the organisation manages, develops and releases the knowledge and full potential of its people at an individual, team-based and organisation-wide level, and plans these activities in order to support its policy and strategy and the effective operation of its processes.

Sub-criterion 3B:
People's knowledge and competencies are identified, developed and sustained.

Areas to address may include:

- *Identifying, classifying and matching people's knowledge and competencies with the organisation's needs;*

- *Developing and using training and development plans to help ensure people match the present and future capability needs of the organisation;*

- *Designing and promoting individual, team and organisational learning opportunities;*

- *Developing people through work experience;*

- *Developing team skills;*

- *Aligning individual and team objectives with the organisation's targets;*

- *Reviewing and updating individual and team objectives;*

- *Appraising and helping people improve their performance.*

PRIVATE SECTOR

To aid motivation individuals are developed through long-term plans. Business, Personal and Stretch objectives are cascaded from the Board on a yearly basis and monitored through quarterly reviews. Personal Development Plans ensure training and mentoring is utilised to best benefit the individual and the business, and controlled through a training and development budget.

We developed the 'Exceeding Expectations' improvement programme as a framework to aid teams achieve our and their business goals and better understand our Mission and Values. Teams work through the nine modules designed to promote the value of both our internal and external customers. Ensuring the programme works, we have designed a Mentoring Support Loop allowing team ideas to be visibly encouraged by the Board. The Exceeding Expectations programme has proved to be a success and will shortly be rolled out to the Group.

Feedback is critical so various forums have been created allowing ground-level staff the opportunity to impact upon the workings of the Division. Annually, a group of staff review the Vision, Mission and Values with the Savings Board to ensure all our Stakeholders needs are being addressed this also demonstrates staff involvement and not just management words.

Staff development is also monitored through Staff and Customer Perception surveys. Emphasis on these two Stakeholders is achieved through regularly reviewed growth targets.

Links to Fundamental Concepts

☑ Leadership and constancy of purpose	☐ Customer focus
	☐ Partner development
☐ Management by process and facts	☐ Public responsibility
☑ People development and involvement	☐ Results orientation
☑ Continuous learning, improvement and innovation	

Our Personal Development Review system is fundamental to the preservation and development of our people's skills and is an integral part of Human Resource policy. This allows our people to develop personal and management skills by agreeing training requirements on a Personal Development Plan. In December 1998, after consultation with people throughout the business, we introduced Personal Development Portfolios to focus people on their personal development and allow them the opportunity to record examples of the competences they have demonstrated. Our skills requirements are determined by the tasks our customers demand of us and the expected volumes/nature of work. Short and long-term needs are defined and reviewed by our Human Resource Team. Competence profiles, which include teamwork, forward thinking and interpersonal skills, are required for every job within the organisation.

The Human Resource Manager in consultation with Business Unit managers aligns an individual's skills with job competence profiles and business needs. Profiles ensure that an individual's skills are matched with the post. This enables jobholders to compare their skills with those required for a particular post and identify short and longer-term training needs for inclusion in Personnel Development Plans. We continuously develop skills by researching and investing in new training programmes aligned to future business needs.

The annual Staff Training and Development Strategic Plan ensures alignment between business objectives, future capability and individual development needs. The annual Training and Development Plan sets out the training priorities and developmental needs to meet organisational objectives and the individual needs of our people as identified with their managers in their Personnel Development Plans.

SMALL/MEDIUM

One area we do excel in is the training element, which has been supported by the company winning a National Investors Peoples Award. The adoption of the Business Excellence Model process has ensured we operate a structured approach to training. The approach is reviewed annually by the company and every three years by Investors in People.

This process allows us to review our short and long term business and 'skills needs' from our Strategic Architecture (3–5 year rolling business plan). The short term includes Employee Appraisals, Local and Legislative needs, which is transformed into one annual plan. This plan is reviewed and adjusted quarterly to accommodate the ongoing business flexibility needs. The process requires participation at all levels of the organisation. To improve the effectiveness of the process, we have found that a six-month evaluation of training has been very effective as it allows Managers to review those training plans they have instigated.

This system easily allows us to verify the three stages of evaluation:
(1) that the training achieved its objectives on the day of training
(2) six monthly review shows if the training is being used and is therefore an investment (or needs review or refresher)
(3) it shows the progress to our plan and how it affects the business results and if training has been delivered effectively and its impact on the bottom-line. For example, in 1998 we combined
(i) the introduction of Lean Manufacturing
(ii) introduction of Self-Directed Work Teams on the shop floor
(iii) Kaizen Workshops.
This resulted in a 40% increase in production with the same number of employees, capacity and floor space. We have also continued to grow 20% approximately each year subsequently.

Links to Fundamental Concepts

- ☑ Leadership and constancy of purpose
- ☐ Management by process and facts
- ☑ People development and involvement
- ☑ Continuous learning, improvement and innovation
- ☐ Customer focus
- ☐ Partner development
- ☐ Public responsibility
- ☐ Results orientation

Links to Fundamental Concepts

- ☑ Leadership and constancy of purpose
- ☐ Management by process and facts
- ☑ People development and involvement
- ☑ Continuous learning, improvement and innovation
- ☐ Customer focus
- ☐ Partner development
- ☐ Public responsibility
- ☐ Results orientation

Criterion 3

3.3 | People

How the organisation manages, develops and releases the knowledge and full potential of its people at an individual, team-based and organisation-wide level, and plans these activities in order to support its policy and strategy and the effective operation of its processes.

Sub-criterion 3C:
People are involved and empowered.

Areas to address may include:

- *Encouraging and supporting individual and team participation in improvement activities;*

- *Encouraging and supporting people's involvement through in-house conferences and ceremonies;*

- *Providing opportunities that stimulate involvement and support innovative and creative behaviour;*

- *Empowering people to take action;*

- *Encouraging people to work together in teams.*

PRIVATE SECTOR

Team working and ongoing improvement have been core aspects of our culture since the late 1970s. In that period it has developed from gaining commitment to team work as an appropriate way of working, through developing expertise in the use of quality tools for improvement, to its present-day form of (Small Improvement Groups) and (Small Project Groups). Involvement is gained through the employee performance review process which reviews past performance, future objectives, upward feedback on his or her direct leader and the identification of future development needs and 87% of staff participated.

Small Improvement Groups play a significant part in gaining involvement of people and promoting taking of responsibility for solving problems. Small Improvement Groups enable individuals or small groups to identify small improvement opportunities (kaizen) and, following agreement with the Department Manager/Supervisor, implementing the improvements. The more substantial improvements are managed via the focus charts discussed. Over 1000 Small Improvement Groups have been recorded each year. Other activities enable groups of 3–6 employees to tackle a significant improvement opportunity. Normally management directed, a Team Leader will be designated (at operator or Team Leader who will then pull together an appropriate mix of skills to tackle the project. About 25 groups are active each year, producing improvements that typically run into six figure sums.

Each year, a plant presentation day is held which involves teams from each Department presenting their themes to the whole of the organisation. The best team receives a small prize, and all team members who participated receive a special group badge, which can only be worn by those individuals who have been involved with a theme completion. Every two years the top team from each of the two preceding years will take part in a special competition, the winners of which visit the Parent Company in Japan, where they present their achievements to the directors and employees.

Links to Fundamental Concepts

☑ Leadership and constancy of purpose

☐ Management by process and facts

☑ People development and involvement

☑ Continuous learning, improvement and innovation

☐ Customer focus

☐ Partner development

☐ Public responsibility

☐ Results orientation

PUBLIC SECTOR

People can choose which School Improvement Group they wish to join. Senior leaders help in the planning, monitoring and review of the work of the groups. The School Development Committee outlined the methodology for deciding on improvement activities and this is made available to all staff. The work of School Improvement Groups is given a high profile on staff training days. New recruits are encouraged to join the Senior Management Team.

Our mission of "Excellence" embraces the concept of teamwork and involvement of everyone.

All staff are consulted and /or actively involved in the drawing up of policy and strategy and in their review. This provides opportunities for all levels of staff to demonstrate innovative and creative behaviour, e.g. in reviewing the strategy on Discipline, staff asked for a School Improvement Group to be set up to look at ways of rewarding pupils for good behaviour. This was done and 7 excellent ideas resulted. These have been implemented and will be monitored and reviewed by the Pastoral team and the School Discipline Committee.

Heads of Year can decide what action to take regarding pupil discipline, without having to refer their decisions to the next line of management. They can also monitor and review their actions without further referral. Likewise, Heads of Department can decide their own teaching strategies, implement, monitor and review them without referral to the next line of management, e.g., a Mathematics teacher introduced a new strategy of individualised learning for teaching 'A' level Mathematics. He planned, implemented, monitored and reviewed it through the performance of the pupils. Evaluation of people empowerment and effectiveness takes place on a two yearly basis, e.g. as a result of review, it was decided to empower teachers to develop their own Literacy strategies within their departments and to share these with the whole staff.

Teamwork is an integral part of our way of doing things.

Links to Fundamental Concepts

- ☑ Leadership and constancy of purpose
- ☐ Management by process and facts
- ☑ People development and involvement
- ☑ Continuous learning, improvement and innovation
- ☐ Customer focus
- ☐ Partner development
- ☐ Public responsibility
- ☐ Results orientation

SMALL/MEDIUM

It is critical to our success that everyone is firstly able to contribute the best of their abilities and secondly feels involved in continuing improving the performance of the business. Indeed our Quality Policy outlines the key role employees place in our pursuit of excellence.

The execution of this policy is communicated via the corporate refresher inductions. Feedback is reviewed and corrective action taken.

It is vital, to encourage employee involvement and engagement, that regularly pull people together to share business progress and priorities and celebrate success where appropriate. We are constantly striving to be first to market with new concepts and product innovations. This year's survey showed that 97% of employees felt that they had the freedom to make suggestions for new products, systems and solutions to problems.

Empowerment of our people is essential for us to keep pace with customer needs, make timely decisions and contribute to the development of the business. This is encouraged through team meeting and cross-functional focus groups. In team meetings any initiatives or other business discussed at Management Meetings is cascaded to other team members. In addition, the enabling technology of the business empowers people to a great extent. For instance, new technology gives the trading teams great visibility of profitability – they are empowered to make decisions based on this; plus Lotus Notes provides the technical mechanism for trading teams to submit tactical proposals.

This year's survey showed that 85% of employees felt that they are free to do the things they are capable of.

Teamwork is also now on the agenda for off-site meetings where activities are undertaken to help foster teamwork. For example, at the Wholesale & Convenience quarterly sales meeting external consultants were used in the running of a number of team building exercises. The recent employee survey showed that 76% of employees feel that their team skills are being developed.

Links to Fundamental Concepts

- ☑ Leadership and constancy of purpose
- ☐ Management by process and facts
- ☑ People development and involvement
- ☑ Continuous learning, improvement and innovation
- ☐ Customer focus
- ☐ Partner development
- ☐ Public responsibility
- ☐ Results orientation

Criterion 3

3.3 | People

H ow the organisation manages, develops and releases the knowledge and full potential of its people at an individual, team-based and organisation-wide level, and plans these activities in order to support its policy and strategy and the effective operation of its processes.

Sub-criterion 3D:

People and the organisation have a dialogue.

Areas to address may include:

- *Identifying communication needs;*

- *Developing communications policies, strategies and plans based on communications needs;*

- *Developing and using top down, bottom up and horizontal communication channels;*

- *Sharing best practice and knowledge.*

PRIVATE SECTOR

Communication is a key part of the success of our business. Identifying communication needs is not just about understanding what people want to know, but is also about determining what they need to know to enable them to perform better. Further it is about understanding what the business needs to know from its people. The information on communication needs is gathered through a variety of approaches including:

Performance Appraisal and Career and Personal Development Reviews: Through discussion with line managers associates highlight the supporting information they need to have communicated to them to do their jobs. Equally the line manager establishes the communication they need from their associates.

Daily Briefs: The Daily Briefs as well as providing the communication vehicle, also identify the needs with associates deciding on the subjects they wish to discuss.

Surveys: Questions within the surveys identify the areas where associates believe they are not getting enough information (or perhaps too much!).

Team Meetings: Again agendas are influenced by the needs of the associates.

Feedback on Events: The feedback on communication events enables us to identify shortfalls in the communication.

Strategic Planning: Where the corporate communication strategies are determined and defined.

Marketing Strategy: Where the internal communications regarding new products/services special promotions etc are determined and designed.

Executive Teams: Where communication strategies are determined. The range of communication channels is considerable. They include Corporate Communication Vehicles such as: Business Plan and Balanced Scorecard available to all associates.

Weekly Bulletin: If any information is to be distributed to all hotels the information is gathered together and sent in a weekly brief.

Links to Fundamental Concepts

☑ Leadership and constancy of purpose	☐ Customer focus
	☐ Partner development
☐ Management by process and facts	☐ Public responsibility
☑ People development and involvement	☐ Results orientation
☐ Continuous learning, improvement and innovation	

PUBLIC SECTOR

Communication is an extremely important aspect of any business and the department realises this and as a result has its own Communication manager to ensure that staff are aware of important issues.

The department called upon a communications consultant to improve communications within the business unit, the consultant held workshops with over 101 staff and provided advice to staff on communications issues. A training event was held to develop skills in managing change and to introduce a communications planning process.

The communications manager has set up a forum where staff from each area of the business take forward ideas, issues and problems to allow for a better communication system within the department. Staff are also involved in a variety of forums such as the Green Commuting Working Party and Appropriate behaviour workshops, providing staff with the opportunity to put forward their ideas and views and views of the colleagues that they represent.

Quality hours are a weekly event for every team on every command and provide staff with the opportunity to discuss issues around work. It is often in quality hour that Team Briefs are delivered, and other important documents are cascaded to our staff. This hour is seen as a communication tool and gives line managers the freedom to innovate during these meetings, for example some team leaders hold team-building events in this hour whilst others discuss methods of improving productivity. This promotes feedback from staff enabling them to have input into the way they work.

There are numerous notice boards around the department displaying various information from details of events to information regarding our computer system.

Links to Fundamental Concepts

☑ Leadership and constancy of purpose

☐ Management by process and facts

☑ People development and involvement

☐ Continuous learning, improvement and innovation

☐ Customer focus

☐ Partner development

☐ Public responsibility

☐ Results orientation

SMALL/MEDIUM

Our strategy was developed to give direction and guidance to our people enabling communication vehicles to be tailored to best meet the needs of each of the purposes. A clear aspect of the strategy is to engender a philosophy of constant challenge and review, where individuals are encouraged to question communication processes and in particular their own responsibilities to ensure communication is as effective and direct as possible.

Employee feedback and discussion on communication effectiveness has enabled us to continually review our strategy. Discussion within our Intranet Authors Group, a session on communication within our refresher induction programmes and specific questions via the employee surveys has brought about changes to what were previously considered effective communication channels. We use a variety of communication methods, such as: tea meetings, the Intranet, e-mail, informal meetings, team briefs, phone calls, and management meetings.

The need for a central forum for key information and the sophistication of our systems has enabled the development of the Intranet. It carries information on a variety of subjects, in a very user friendly format Simple navigation enables access to areas split into People, Process Brands, Customers, Consumers, Info and Results, and External Links. A survey showed that over 75% of employees access the Intranet at least daily.

Each year we undertake an exercise to establish our headcount for the coming year based on business needs. Should a situation arise where we are over our headcount then this is managed in a fair and consistent way.

For those who were leaving our business, counselling feedback sessions were given and a full brief on their redundancy package guidelines and other support given such as outplacement career counselling and the opportunity to purchase their company car at a reduced rate. We also undertook discussions to identify any possible job opportunities.

Links to Fundamental Concepts

☑ Leadership and constancy of purpose

☐ Management by process and facts

☐ People development and involvement

☐ Continuous learning, improvement and innovation

☐ Customer focus

☐ Partner development

☐ Public responsibility

☐ Results orientation

Criterion 3

3.3 | People

H ow the organisation manages,
develops and releases the
knowledge and full potential of its
people at an individual, team-based
and organisation-wide level, and
plans these activities in order to
support its policy and strategy and
the effective operation of its processes.

> **Sub-criterion 3E:**
> People are rewarded, recognised
> and cared for.

Areas to address may include:

- *Aligning remuneration, redeployment,
  redundancy and other terms of
  employment with policy and strategy;*

- *Recognising people in order to
  sustain their involvement
  and empowerment;*

- *Promoting awareness and
  involvement in health, safety,
  the environment and issues on
  social responsibility;*

- *Setting the levels of benefits,
  e.g. pension plan, health care,
  child care;*

- *Promoting social and cultural activities.*

- *Providing facilities and services,
  e.g. flexible hours, transport.*

PRIVATE SECTOR The organisation has excellent focus on People and People Results. Yearly a 'People' survey known as CARE and this year called 'Our Place to Work' is conducted. Everyone in the organisation is encouraged to complete the survey, this year it was on-line. The results are reviewed in all the teams, action plans are produced to address key areas and a monthly confidence index is carried out from a random sample of people to check progress.

Comprehensive training programmes are implemented when this is seen as a key area to improve and a new reward and recognition scheme was implemented to also address a key area. To ensure issues are raised and actions are taken a 'whiteboard' process was implemented. This is just that, a whiteboard is used at every team meeting across the organisation to gather issues and the issues stay on the board until addressed.

Links to Fundamental Concepts

☑ Leadership and constancy of purpose ☐ Customer focus
☐ Management by process and facts ☐ Partner development
☐ People development and involvement ☐ Public responsibility
☐ Continuous learning, improvement and innovation ☑ Results orientation

Criterion 3

PUBLIC SECTOR

The Pupils committee considers pastoral issues, and the committee meets every term. The Committee reviewed and updated, as necessary, policies relating to pastoral issues. The focus of our work was in reviewing the behaviour of our students towards each other, the staff, and the processes that have been implemented. The Positive Behaviour Plan linked with our policy against bullying is at the core of this work. This is an area that requires a high degree of consistency in policy implementation if both students and staff are to recognise improvements in the environment where teachers can teach, and students can learn.

Students have made significant progress in the overall standard of student behaviour through the efforts of staff, and acceptance of the good behaviour principles. The principles, classroom responsibilities, behaviour consequences, advice and behaviour outside the classroom are clearly documented for the teaching staff and pupils. This is a very positive plan that is aimed at changing behaviour with reward, praise and acknowledgement.

Rewards can be Lottery tickets – ten per tutor group per term, Year group merits, form prizes. Sanctions can include break time detention, letter home to parents, and no school trips.

The school enjoys a well-earned reputation for the range and quality of additional activities and learning opportunities for pupils. Every pupil should be able to find an interest in which to participate, outside of the normal school day. Of course, a number of these activities give the opportunity for parents and family to witness the success of the pupils, e.g. music concerts, drama productions and dance productions, all of which enhance pupils' confidence, and create a working together environment.

We are very appreciative of the amount of hard work, personal time and dedication of staff that organise these and the other many activities, and of course the enthusiasm of the pupils, and the support of parents.

Links to Fundamental Concepts

- ☑ Leadership and constancy of purpose
- ☐ Management by process and facts
- ☐ People development and involvement
- ☐ Continuous learning, improvement and innovation
- ☐ Customer focus
- ☐ Partner development
- ☐ Public responsibility
- ☑ Results orientation

SMALL/MEDIUM

We have a number of strategies and policies to support people in our business with regard to how they are rewarded, recognised and cared for.

We use a job evaluation system to ensure that roles are sized consistently and fairly, and with uniformity across the company. This allows us to match a salary range to the job grade. Our salaries are benchmarked to ensure we are within the top quartile, against a range of Nation Surveys. Individual salaries are audited each spring by the Remuneration Department across the Company, and, for example, anomalies to mark rate are highlighted. Each autumn we undertake an annual salary review where awards are linked to performance. Plus, we practice active salary management by addressing salary issues as they arise.

Equal opportunities are addressed in this area also. Within the last few months an audit has been conducted across the company to assess gender bias.

We also operate a profit related bonus scheme applicable to all employees that allows a bonus payout based on percentage of salary should profit targets be achieved.

An incentive scheme is also run for the sales team where award is has not solely on individual achievement but by team achievement as well.

Centrally, a Remuneration Committee operates at plc level benchmarking our remuneration and benefits, and guidelines are then passed down to individual trading companies. A Remuneration Working Party is in place at local level to ensure consistency of application of policies and to address any issues.

Through employee surveys and line management input, employees are given the opportunity to comment on remuneration and benefits and this feedback is then addressed.

All employees receive full details on their employment details, rights entitlements and responsibilities through individual contracts of employment and the Company Management Handbook. As a caring employer our target is to succeed statutory requirements for our people policies, such as in our provision of redundancy payments and support.

Links to Fundamental Concepts

- ☑ Leadership and constancy of purpose
- ☐ Management by process and facts
- ☐ People development and involvement
- ☐ Continuous learning, improvement and innovation
- ☐ Customer focus
- ☐ Partner development
- ☐ Public responsibility
- ☑ Results orientation

Criterion 3

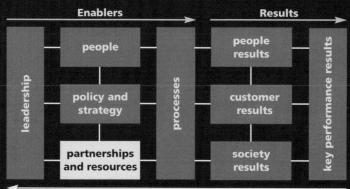

The Excellence Model

Enablers

Results

leadership

people

policy and
strategy

processes

partnerships
and resources

people
results

customer
results

society
results

key performance results

Innovation and Learning

© 1999 EFQM.

"The organisation's internal resources (e.g. assets) and external resources (e.g. suppliers) are managed to ensure its policy and strategy can be delivered."

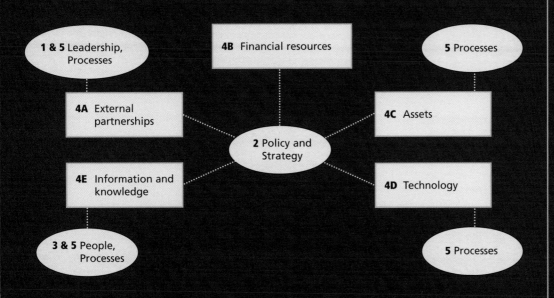

Linkages between the sub-criteria and with the other enablers

3.4 | Partnerships and Resources

How the organisation plans and manages its external partnerships and internal resources in order to support its policy and strategy and the effective operation of its processes.

Sub-criterion 4A:
External partnerships are managed.

Areas to address may include:

- *Identifying key partners and strategic partnership opportunities in line with policy and strategy;*

- *Structuring partnership relationships to create and maximise value;*

- *Forming value-adding supply chain partnerships;*

- *Ensuring cultural compatibility and the sharing of knowledge with partner organisations;*

- *Supporting mutual development;*

- *Generating and supporting innovative and creative thinking through the use of partnerships;*

- *Creating synergy in working together to improve processes and add value to the customer/supplier chain.*

PRIVATE SECTOR

Our business unit is a smaller unit of a larger group. As such the supply of items into us is dictated by the organisational structure. Nevertheless, we take a degree of control of these partnerships as internal customers.

Our policy and strategy drive our approach to supplier relationships. This is realised by working with suppliers to deliver components to required quality and to plan, so reducing total programme lead times and costs. We aim to strengthen our key partnerships through a reduction in the number of relationships.

As an operational unit within a group, our closest partners are the Outside Business Units. This partnership is driven by the common Enterprise Resource Planning system, recently installed across the company. Our controllers place orders on to the Outside Business Units in line with the demand through the system.

In the product development phase, many of our engineers work closely with their Outside Business Units colleagues to define the tools and equipment needed for the operations unit processes. A review of the issues raised has resulted in "working together" sessions on Design for Assembly for the new projects.

Our process improvement teams work with our partners to produce a mutually beneficial solution, e.g. integrated work patterns meant reusable packaging saved warehousing, handling and unpacking time throughout the process.

Our supply chain's largely specified at the outset of any engine project. Both internal supply and special providers have to be integrated into our business supply chain and we work closely with them to ensure compliance with our needs.

Links to Fundamental Concepts

- ☐ Leadership and constancy of purpose
- ☐ Customer focus
- ☐ Management by process and facts
- ☑ Partner development
- ☐ People development and involvement
- ☐ Public responsibility
- ☐ Continuous learning, improvement and innovation
- ☐ Results orientation

Criterion 4

PUBLIC SECTOR

"Partnership" is one of our core values. The quality of our partnerships has been recognised in our being one of only 3 award winners the TNT Modernising Government Partnerships Awards 2000. We have also received 3 nationally recognised Schools Curriculum Awards, the latest to be presented in June 2000 for the quality of our partnerships with parents and community. We want to deliver our critical and enabling processes in an environment of partnership that emphasises social inclusiveness and where joined-up services ensure that every pupil is given the best possible chance to achieve. This approach is absolutely crucial especially for a school such as ours in a highly deprived area. Each year, in the review of our School Action Plan, we identify our key partners for the coming year.

We may, for example, decide to continue with particular primary schools and scale-down our partnership with others if we feel that the partnership is no longer adding value.

All suppliers have a contact name in the school. This usually is a member of support staff who is much more accessible than teaching staff. Contact can be made with a teacher by arrangement through our clerical staff or by prior appointment. Complaints are very rare and queries are dealt with as far as possible on the same day.

There are complaints procedures in place and these are available to our customers as well as our suppliers but they have yet to be used by our suppliers. This is most definitely due to the very efficient work of our office staff who respond immediately to suppliers' concerns. Our pro-active involvement with our suppliers is realised in terms of surveys, interviews, informal talks, participation in school improvements and the formulation of a set of guarantees for our suppliers.

SMALL/MEDIUM

As our business has grown, our approach has been to develop partnership relationships that are mutually beneficial. Our Strategic Plan identifies the kind of partnerships that we seek to create and examples of these can be found throughout the Company.

For example, the Company has a long-standing partnership with a software provider and we have worked together to develop a Certificate of Competence, the profits of which are divided between the two companies. Another example of partnership working can be found in the Accessible Excellence team where an innovative project has resulted in the development of a portfolio of partnerships – a group of high quality suppliers whose products we are to distribute to our specialized customer base at a rate, which will also provide us with an income.

We also have a close working relationship with another of our partners who have been responsible for producing the written content of our work based learning material. Our Company has shared our ideas for the future to see whether there are any areas to exploit that could be mutually beneficial.

One of the key benefits to arise from our partnership relationships has been improved customer satisfaction and refined processes. Our customer evaluation process indicated that we needed to invest in giving a greater degree of feedback to students and in establishing a partnership between this Company and a group of external assessors we have been able to meet these needs. We have organised special training days for the assessors and have a programme in place to review the quality of the work carried out by them.

Links to Fundamental Concepts

☐ Leadership and constancy of purpose

☐ Management by process and facts

☐ People development and involvement

☐ Continuous learning, improvement and innovation

☐ Customer focus

☑ Partner development

☐ Public responsibility

☐ Results orientation

Links to Fundamental Concepts

☐ Leadership and constancy of purpose

☐ Management by process and facts

☐ People development and involvement

☐ Continuous learning, improvement and innovation

☐ Customer focus

☑ Partner development

☐ Public responsibility

☐ Results orientation

Criterion 4

3.4 Partnerships and Resources

H ow the organisation plans and manages its external partnerships and internal resources in order to support its policy and strategy and the effective operation of its processes.

Sub-criterion 4B:
Finances are managed.

Areas to address may include:

- *Using financial resources in support of policy and strategy;*

- *Developing and implementing financial strategies and processes;*

- *Evaluating investment in both tangible and non-tangible assets;*

- *Using financial mechanisms and parameters to ensure an efficient and effective resourcing structure;*

- *Managing risks to financial resources.*

PRIVATE SECTOR

In addition to competing for market share, we must also compete for investors to fund future growth. Our ability to attract investors was the subject of a 1996 study using consultants from the financial sector. This resulted in the decision to focus our Strategic Business Units on improving performance based on Earnings Before Interest and Tax, reflecting the profitability of the company in terms of profits generated before interest and tax and Economic Value Added which is a measure of the degree to which the returns generated exceed the cost of financing the assets employed. Our driver tree provides a guide for financial management. There are clear linkages between the Economic Value Added driver tree and our strategic themes. This approach for linking strategy to action is recognised as best in class by many organisations including the EFQM.

The construction of plans for the allocation of financial resources in support of policy and strategy is an integral part of the Strategic Planning Process. Plans are required for all significant activities carried out within the business. These are consolidated at business level following review and agreement of divisional level plans, and facilitate top level resource and organisational planning; capital investment planning; and overall financial planning.

The consolidation of these plans and iterative review and approval provides a mechanism to link the management of financial resources with our financial strategy. The Balanced Scorecard process ensures that the impact of financial decisions on Process, Innovation and Customer Satisfaction is taken into account and decisions are not made solely on the basis of short-term financial goals. The extent to which financial resources are used to support strategy is subject to continuous Situation Appraisal in every quadrant of the balanced scorecard.

Links to Fundamental Concepts

☑ Leadership and constancy of purpose	☐ Customer focus
	☐ Partner development
☐ Management by process and facts	☐ Public responsibility
☐ People development and involvement	☑ Results orientation
☑ Continuous learning, improvement and innovation	

Criterion 4

PUBLIC SECTOR Our financial policies are derived from legislation, the Chartered Institute of Public Finance and Accountancy Best Value Accounting Code of Practice, the County Council's Financial Regulations and to directly support policy and strategy. The council's financial regulations are currently under review to which we have made our recommendations for change. Similarly, we contribute towards the council's response to consultation on legislation and the Code of Practice.

Finance is managed through the corporate ledger and divisional management information systems. Our Finance and Commercial Manager, a qualified accountant, owns and reports upon the financial management system to the Directorate Management Team. The Director of Finance supports the corporate financial system. All systems are subject to independent review by the authority's Chief Internal Auditor and external auditor. Until the repeal of compulsory competitive tendering in January 2001, they were also subject to inspection by the Department of the Environment, Transport and the Regions.

The Finance and Commercial Manager reports to Directorate Management Team on the Financial Strategy and this is reviewed, along with any recommendations from internal and external audit, at the Annual Strategic Workshop to ensure alignment with policy and strategy. Operational Services Committee oversees the whole process, with the Finance and Commercial Manager presenting quarterly reports on the financial performance of each division and the Directorate overall. Members are thus given the opportunity to challenge and comment upon our financial management.

Directorate objectives are agreed through incorporation of annual budgets built up by division, service, area and overhead accounts. Financial targets are thus established along with the key tasks necessary to achieve them.

 SMALL/MEDIUM Our financial strategy forms a key part of our strategic planning system and key financial goals are identified and understood by all staff via strategic planning wall charts which are displayed across the entire Company. The Company was formed not only to support individual students and employers but also to generate income for the College itself and this requirement is at the forefront of our financial strategy and is well understood by all employees.

Financial management and reporting follows the organisational structure. Each team has its own budget and teams' financial records are managed and updated by team budget co-ordinators. Our Finance Team Leader collates information from team records monthly and a report is prepared for the Chief Executive detailing gross profit, turnover, cash flow etc. This information is used to assist our understanding of our progress and to inform decisions about bonus payments. We formally review our performance against our profit targets monthly and information regarding performance in relation to goal sharing is also shared with staff monthly.

All of our financial procedures are subject to audit and scrutiny by a number of sources. We are open to examination by our parent organisation, and our financial processes comply with their requirements and are audited by internal auditors. In addition, our financial processes are audited annually. However, our financial systems are also subject to annual audit by the Further Education Funding Council, as assurance needs to be given that the company is claiming the correct amount of funding for work carried out. Our Finance Team leader therefore continually reviews our processes to ensure that the information recorded is robust.

Links to Fundamental Concepts

- ☐ Leadership and constancy of purpose
- ☑ Management by process and facts
- ☐ People development and involvement
- ☐ Continuous learning, improvement and innovation
- ☐ Customer focus
- ☐ Partner development
- ☐ Public responsibility
- ☑ Results orientation

Links to Fundamental Concepts

- ☐ Leadership and constancy of purpose
- ☑ Management by process and facts
- ☐ People development and involvement
- ☐ Continuous learning, improvement and innovation
- ☐ Customer focus
- ☐ Partner development
- ☐ Public responsibility
- ☑ Results orientation

Criterion 4

3.4 | Partnerships and Resources

How the organisation plans and manages its external partnerships and internal resources in order to support its policy and strategy and the effective operation of its processes.

Sub-criterion 4C:
Buildings, equipment and materials are managed.

Areas to address may include:

- *Utilising assets in support of policy and strategy;*

- *Managing the maintenance and utilisation of assets to improve total asset life cycle performance;*

- *Managing the security of assets;*

- *Measuring and managing any adverse effects of the organisation's assets on the community and employees (including health and safety);*

- *Optimising material inventories;*

- *Optimising consumption of utilities;*

- *Reducing and recycling waste;*

- *Conserving global non-renewable resources;*

- *Reducing any adverse global impact of products and services.*

PRIVATE SECTOR

We are responsible for the management of assembly and test facilities. We dedicate an amount per annum to the maintenance and running of these facilities. This amount covers the personnel involved, payments to our partners as well as maintenance materials.

Organisational review created Assembly and Test organisations, which facilitated the pooling of experimental and production facilities and equipment. The planning process now utilises the full range of capability within the Group. This includes our workforce, which is trained and utilised for development and production activities.

The overall utilisation of the facilities is reviewed at quarterly intervals within the financial review, based on the longer-range plans of our customers. This review considers all the facilities available, including those at other sites as well as at our partner companies in Japan and Spain. Other factors are also included in this review such as the impact of the testing schedules on the local community. Action is taken where opportunities can be identified to improve utilisation, fully recognising issues such as noise. If the review shows up potential risks to the plans of then a formal risk review is completed, resulting in plans to address the major issues.

Assets in use in the unit are either owned by the 'landlord' or by the unit directly. Where these are directly owned they are assigned to a department for depreciation charges. Many of these assets are of high value and to achieve efficient use of this investment they are operated up to 24 hours a day. The owning department is responsible for the maintenance of the asset.

The company has the responsibility for maintaining buildings and providing architectural and planning services. Maintenance levels applied to buildings are linked to their role in the site plan and their planned life.

Links to Fundamental Concepts

- ☐ Leadership and constancy of purpose
- ☑ Management by process and facts
- ☐ People development and involvement
- ☐ Continuous learning, improvement and innovation
- ☐ Customer focus
- ☐ Partner development
- ☐ Public responsibility
- ☐ Results orientation

PUBLIC SECTOR

The school maximises the use of all classrooms including specialist rooms such as Information Technology, Science, Music in order to ensure that we deliver our critical process, Teaching and Learning as efficiently and effectively as possible. In support of our enabling process, we open the school to the community 5 evenings per week during which time, it is used by parents and groups such as Scouts, Unislim, and a Mother and Toddler Group. It is also used for Saturday School, from 10.00 a.m. – 1.00 p.m. for our own pupils, and from 2.00 p.m. – 4.00 p.m. for pupils from our feeder primary schools.

All of these people are able to make use of the resources in the school after school hours. The School is open to pupils for a Homework Club and to many others for after school activities. We hold special study weekends, e.g., a Science weekend, and during the Easter holidays we hold a study week.

We review the process for the management of assets in addressing the effectiveness of our critical process, Teaching and Learning, on an annual basis. Review takes place at Head of Department level and following review, amendments are made and implemented, e.g. a review of the use of text-books was carried out by the History Department which addressed the cost of photo-copying text-books as an alternative to ordering new copies. Following review, it was found to be more cost-effective to order new books. A plan was drawn up by the department to order a specified number of textbooks from each year's departmental budget.

We manage the maintenance and utilisation of assets through a Resources Management Strategy that is followed by all budget holders. We also use a range of measures to protect valuable assets which include the following:
- an annual audit of equipment undertaken by the Audio Visual Technician
- a strong room for the storing of valuable assets, e.g. camcorders, cameras
- books in the library are security-tagged
- pupils pay deposits to borrow musical instruments, e.g. pupils pay £10 deposits to have guitars in the Folk Music Club.

Links to Fundamental Concepts

- ☐ Leadership and constancy of purpose
- ☑ Management by process and facts
- ☐ People development and involvement
- ☐ Continuous learning, improvement and innovation
- ☐ Customer focus
- ☐ Partner development
- ☐ Public responsibility
- ☐ Results orientation

SMALL/MEDIUM

We moved into our current premises in March 1998 as part of a planned expansion. The building is leased and an Estates Management Company has overall responsibility for the external fabric of the building. Internal repairs are managed by this company in line with established procurement processes. Comprehensive security policies are in place to protect our assets, e.g. alarm system and password controlled door access. All staff are given guidance about these procedures at induction stage. A security-working group has also been established to achieve the BS7799 Information Security Management Standard.

The College controls the recording and management of our Company assets and they also calculate depreciation values.

IT systems are properly maintained with regular back-ups taken. There has only been one recorded Incident of our computer systems failing (down time only lasting 15mins) in the Company's history.

An innovative system is in place for the procurement of our work-based learning materials in that a printing company stores our stock and delivers our materials within two working days. This enables the Company to limit the amount of stock holding on the premises to 25% of available materials, which maximises our use of space.

An accident reporting system is in place to measure the impact of the organisation on the health and well being of staff. Health and Safety representatives are in place in all parts of the organisation and this team keep an advice board up-to-date with guidelines and advice on Health and Safety matters.

The Company is also highly and visibly committed to conserving global non-renewable resources. Recycling points exist in the main access to the building for cans, glass, paper and newspapers and staff enthusiastically supports these.

Links to Fundamental Concepts

- ☐ Leadership and constancy of purpose
- ☑ Management by process and facts
- ☐ People development and involvement
- ☐ Continuous learning, improvement and innovation
- ☐ Customer focus
- ☐ Partner development
- ☐ Public responsibility
- ☑ Results orientation

Criterion 4

3.4 | Partnerships and Resources

How the organisation plans and manages its external partnerships and internal resources in order to support its policy and strategy and the effective operation of its processes.

Sub-criterion 4D:
Technology is managed.

Areas to address may include:

- *Identifying and evaluating alternative and emerging technologies in the light of policy and strategy, and their impact on the organisation and society;*

- *Managing the technology portfolio;*

- *Exploiting existing technology;*

- *Innovating technology;*

- *Harnessing technology to support improvement;*

- *Identifying and replacing 'old' technologies.*

PRIVATE SECTOR

Our business strategy and review has a considerable focus on technology and Information Systems, as these play significant roles in how we supply services to and communicate with our customers.

We identify our technology needs through the business planning process and work with our technology partners and IT system providers to exploit technology to best advantage, to improve our processes and meet our business objectives.

We have a dedicated team IT team who develop our IT strategy. This team, who is managed by a member of our executive team, reviews our hardware and software needs with our partner service provider to provide systems that meet our business and stakeholders needs.

We assess our information resources to provide balance and to meet our aim of providing value for money. All our people who require them have computer terminals with access to all relevant databases, intranet sites and the internet.

We have a mobile phone policy that categorises users into 'Essential User' or 'Frequent User' with suitable call tariffs to match needs. As part of our future strategic needs we have an internet site and each of our business units have their own sites. These sites are linked together to allow ease of movement by our viewers and customers from one site to another.

We have a team of 5 people, headed by a manager, who identify and co-ordinate alternative and emerging technologies and new products that support our strategies and future development of our Networks. This 'Technical Development' team interface with business units and technical managers across the company to ensure purpose and meaning to such. The team identifies suitable new technologies and products through a range of media. From information gleaned, proposed new technologies are tested against our business plans and priorities.

Links to Fundamental Concepts

☐ Leadership and constancy of purpose

☐ Management by process and facts

☐ People development and involvement

☐ Continuous learning, improvement and innovation

☐ Customer focus

☐ Partner development

☐ Public responsibility

☑ Results orientation

PUBLIC SECTOR

Responsibility for our Information Technology strategy is taken at a national level. A review of our approach to Information Technology support in 1996 led to us contracting with EDS to manage our technology portfolio. Our Information Technology partner is responsible for providing Information Technology services that maximise our business performance. EDS is working with us assisting with:

- development of a strategic client case management system
- improving access to our services
- improving management information
- development of our core business Information Technology systems.

Our Regional Information Technology Partnership Liaison Manager (RITPLM) manages the partnership at regional level and acts as a central liaison and advice point; ensures that all requests to initiate or change Information Technology or telephony services fall within the our Information Technology strategy and have a sound business justification.

As a region we are involved in piloting and evaluating new technology and its impact on our customers and our business. Roll-out of new systems involves people across the business and we use our communications cycle to continuously identify Information Technology issues and to feed back to our Information Technology partner through our RITPLM and through national forums attended by our Resource Director and Divisional Resource Director. Line Management System is the support system central to delivery of our Performance Results.

It was designed in collaboration with users and put through a series of pilots to confirm business processes and functionality. The rollout of 16,000 computer terminals to 1,070 offices nationally was completed on schedule in four and a half months in 1996. Evaluation has measured the system's availability at 99.5% at the point of use.

Links to Fundamental Concepts

- ☐ Leadership and constancy of purpose
- ☐ Management by process and facts
- ☐ People development and involvement
- ☑ Continuous learning, improvement and innovation
- ☐ Customer focus
- ☐ Partner development
- ☐ Public responsibility
- ☐ Results orientation

SMALL/MEDIUM

The two main areas where technology is used are business Information Technology and manufacturing equipment. The management of existing manufacturing equipment technology is the responsibility of the manager having that equipment in his work area. They can call on other experts, internally and externally, to keep it functioning efficiently. Improvements are also the managers' responsibility.

When capital expenditure is needed it is considered and controlled through the Corrective Action Request process. Whenever possible, identifiable upgrades are added to the yearly profit plan in anticipation of expenditure. These upgrades, to make the more efficient use of the equipment technology, can be the result of employee recommendation after reference to trade journals or exhibitions or their own ideas aimed at improvements. The Information Technology group manages the existing business technology. They are directly responsible for the specification, installation, maintenance and security of all computer based hardware and software.

The need to consider new and emerging technology is driven both directly as solutions to satisfy Strategic Development plans as well as supporting corporate goals. Each development plan is a driver for determining whether we have an existing technology or need new or emerging technology to support the plan. Each plan has an appointed manager to see it through to completion. Monthly reviews take place on all plans where the status is updated to all plan holders and the progress to plan tracked.

To ensure that any equipment or software is justified and meets existing corporate standards all requests for capital expenditure on new technology have to be approved by the department heads and management via the Corrective Action Request process.

Links to Fundamental Concepts

- ☐ Leadership and constancy of purpose
- ☐ Management by process and facts
- ☐ People development and involvement
- ☐ Continuous learning, improvement and innovation
- ☐ Customer focus
- ☐ Partner development
- ☐ Public responsibility
- ☐ Results orientation

Criterion 4

3.4 | Partnerships and Resources

How the organisation plans and manages its external partnerships and internal resources in order to support its policy and strategy and the effective operation of its processes.

Sub-criterion 4E:
Information and knowledge are managed.

Areas to address may include:

- *Collecting, structuring and managing information and knowledge in support of policy and strategy;*

- *Providing appropriate access, for both internal and external users, to relevant information and knowledge;*

- *Assuring and improving information validity, integrity and security;*

- *Cultivating, developing and protecting unique intellectual property to maximise customer value;*

- *Seeking to acquire, increase and use knowledge effectively;*

- *Generating innovative and creative thinking within the organisation through the use of relevant information and knowledge resources.*

PRIVATE SECTOR

Our approach is for every employee to have access to all systems that are required for them to fulfil their roles effectively. Information codified within our systems can be delivered to any computer running within the system environment. The ratio of personal PCs to employees is very close to 1:1, the small number of manufacturing employees who do not have a personal PC use shared terminals in communal areas. Access is provided according to each users profile following a short login procedure. As the system maintains the information within the network itself, users can log onto any PC within the environment and access their own desktop and personal files. This allows users to operate in any geographic location and be machine independent.

The effective use of knowledge within the organisation is underpinned by its approach of integrating knowledge repositories, and providing widespread access through simple systems interfaces. We employ an extensive range of information acquisition channels all aimed at increasing the amount of useful information available to its employees. Information from these sources is codified and store on our Intranet. Information channels are subject to continual Situation Appraisal as is the effective use that this information is put to by our employees. Actions taken following review include an upgrade of Intranet navigation and search facilities to allow relevant information to be rapidly identified.

Measurement of our approach in this area is provided by feedback from the Employee Opinion Survey. Results show a high level of performance in ensuring that employees have access to the information. Innovative use of Intranet and Internet technologies underpins our approach to making information and knowledge resources accessible for use in the creative thinking process.

Links to Fundamental Concepts

- ☐ Leadership and constancy of purpose
- ☑ Management by process and facts
- ☑ People development and involvement
- ☑ Continuous learning, improvement and innovation
- ☐ Customer focus
- ☐ Partner development
- ☐ Public responsibility
- ☐ Results orientation

Criterion 4

PUBLIC SECTOR

The efficient management of information is core to our organisation particularly since we are located over a number of sites. Critical to this are our corporate IT systems. All relevant staff have access to our key housing management and maintenance systems from all our offices. We operate a group wide e-mailing and scheduling system that promotes fast and efficient communication.

Managing our information has become increasingly complex and over the past year we have been running a project called 'access to information' to refine our data handling processes with the end goal of developing electronic document management. As part of this process we now have a document management strategy. The strategy has mapped the way written data is shared and stored.

Service development hinges on the access to common information and technology. Eight years ago few staff head access to a networked system and most staff shared a PC. Now with all office staff networked we are exploring access to systems via remote links. At the same time we are looking at the best way to develop links with our suppliers, following a successful pilot with some of our maintenance contractors who had direct access to our systems.

Links to Fundamental Concepts

- ☐ Leadership and constancy of purpose
- ☑ Management by process and facts
- ☐ People development and involvement
- ☐ Continuous learning, improvement and innovation
- ☐ Customer focus
- ☐ Partner development
- ☐ Public responsibility
- ☐ Results orientation

SMALL/MEDIUM

All production processes on the factory floor are structure around Quality Standard ISO9002. The Standard Operating Procedures of the Quality Manual are displayed beside each machine and cover Activity, Location, Equipment, Responsibility, Safety, Special Tools and Equipment, Quality Checks and Standards, Methods, Records and Housekeeping. Go/No Go boards for quality control showing examples of acceptable/not acceptable products are displayed at key locations in the factory and updated as quality levels improve. The Standard Operating Procedures and the Standard Administrative Procedures ensure that the knowledge required to carry out all procedures in relation to production and administration is monitored, updated and available for the training and multi-skilling of al relevant employees. The intellectual property of the company is enhanced by the continuous training and improvement activities that are part of the company's key objectives. The satellite series on Theory of Constraints brought innovative thinking to the members of the Executive Team and Management Team, which has been extremely valuable in growing and developing the company.

Our people are encouraged to learn and improve in their skills and abilities as much as possible and to use this knowledge in furthering their own and the company's success. Learning opportunities appear weekly in the form of leaflets sent out by training organisations, universities, government agencies, exhibition promoters etc. These training opportunities are assessed informally by the Executive Team and the Management team for the improved knowledge they will bring to the company and the expected benefits.

Courses such as the Local Enterprise Development Unit Cost Reduction Programme and the Theory of Constraints satellite series have allowed staff to gain knowledge from experts. They have then built on this knowledge by putting what they have learned into practice within the company. For example the use of Theory of Constraints within the company has encouraged all the Management team to think in terms of 'bottlenecks'.

Links to Fundamental Concepts

- ☐ Leadership and constancy of purpose
- ☑ Management by process and facts
- ☑ People development and involvement
- ☑ Continuous learning, improvement and innovation
- ☐ Customer focus
- ☐ Partner development
- ☐ Public responsibility
- ☑ Results orientation

Criterion 4

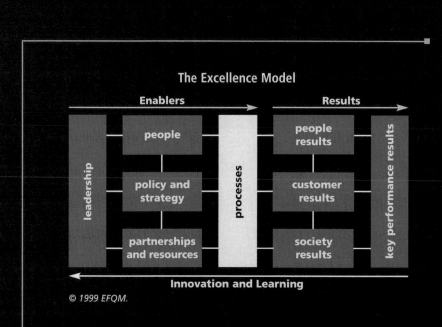

The Excellence Model

Enablers → **Results** →

leadership

people

policy and strategy

partnerships and resources

processes

people results

customer results

society results

key performance results

← **Innovation and Learning**

© 1999 EFQM.

"The organisation has key processes, which are reviewed and improved, to ensure the policy and strategy can be delivered for the benefit of all stakeholders."

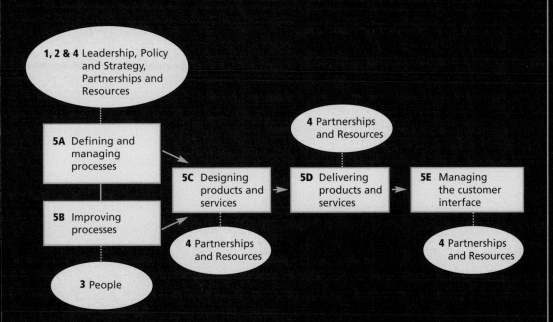

Linkages between
the sub-criteria
and with the
other enablers

3.5 | Processes

H ow the organisation designs, manages and improves its processes in order to support its policy and strategy and fully satisfy, and generate increasing value for, its customers and other stakeholders.

Sub-criterion 5A:

Processes are systematically designed and managed.

Areas to address may include:

- *Designing the organisation's processes, including those key processes needed to deliver policy and strategy;*

- *Establishing the process management system to be used;*

- *Applying systems standards covering, e.g. quality systems such as ISO 9000, environmental systems, occupational health and safety systems in process management;*

- *Implementing process measures and setting performance targets;*

- *Resolving interface issues inside the organisation and with external partners for the effective management of end-to-end processes.*

PRIVATE SECTOR

Process management and design requires a clear understanding of our business aims and what we must deliver to our customers and other stakeholders. To achieve these objectives the then Senior Management Team, in a series of workshops during the last quarter of 1999, identified the value factors that we provide to our customers and the basic value chain needed to deliver them competitively.

The latest review and revision of key processes was undertaken during the strategic 'Challenge' process for 2003, using the feedback from the 1999 UK Quality Award process. This generated a stronger focus on the linkages of the key processes to their core sub-processes through comparison with the value chain and the key deliverables. For the first time, process and functional ownership were agreed. Owning managers became fully accountable to the Manufacturing Director for process performance. Individual policies are set for all key processes, whilst performance indicators, measures and targets are in place to ensure control and reliability. The central policy is the business and plant policy, which provides the focus of our leadership processes. Other policies cascade out to ensure a structured and integrated approach to total operations and support to the customer.

These measures are reviewed and targeted for improvement annually as part of the problem and countermeasure review and incorporated into the annual policy plan. Manufacturing, supplier and customer related measures are set annually by the Quality Manager using an in-company formula based on challenging a minimum 5% improvement on the previous year's performance to drive improvement. In this sense, operational targets are driven by individual and team performance. Indirect process targets are set through consensus by the management team during the policy setting process after discussion with the process owner.

Links to Fundamental Concepts

- ☐ Leadership and constancy of purpose
- ☑ Customer focus
- ☑ Management by process and facts
- ☐ Partner development
- ☐ Public responsibility
- ☐ People development and involvement
- ☐ Results orientation
- ☐ Continuous learning, improvement and innovation

PUBLIC SECTOR

Our approach to process management requires that all our Critical Processes and Sub Processes have appropriate performance measurements, targets and owners in place. We use Quality Improvement Measures to systematically manage our processes. Our Quality Improvement Measure approach is to measure the quality of work 'in-flight'. This system of prevention based process management enables us to take preventative action before tolerance limits are exceeded and begin to impact on customers. We have 2 types of Quality Improvement Measures: short and in-depth. In-depth measures are developed only when the results of our short Quality Improvement Measures point to a procedural difficulty in a particular process. Thus we can quickly identify what stage of the process requires improvement and implement necessary changes. All our processes have Quality Improvement Measures that measure our performance against time, efficiency and accuracy. Individuals have standards and targets for output and quality in their Performance Agreements against which they are assessed through the Performance Management system.

Our process management systems are fully documented in our Business Excellence Guide. Managers and Customer Service Improvement Groups Facilitators in each Business Unit hold copies of the Business Excellence Guide. Process owners establish the standards of operation for our business processes against specific criteria.

Using Business Improvement Plan information and previous years performance figures, managers and staff together agree their key responsibilities and objectives and the criteria for assessment as part of the Performance Management system. Monitoring and reviewing the standards applied to our systems throughout the year is a key part of our Quality Improvement Measurement and Performance Measurement process. Process standards of operation are managed and monitored through Quality Improvement Measures. Quality Improvement Measures are developed in conjunction with the process owner and Quality Development Group.

SMALL/MEDIUM

The use of over 300 flowcharts is the key method for controlling processes. All processes are in a flow chart form in the ISO 9001 "manual" which is stored electronically on the computer network to allow easy access for all. The ISO 9001 system is integral to the success of the Total Quality system. The company's processes are very precise and carefully controlled. This is more so than for many companies because of the requirements for Medical Devices and the American, Food and Drug Administration regulations. An important over-riding factor is that the system is "alive", is regularly updated and includes all aspects of the operation. The administration processes are just as important as the production processes.

The Feedback report following our 1999 UK Business Excellence Award submission was helpful in identifying that we were not maximising our deployment of flowcharts. We now have a far more rigorous approach and the Technical Manager makes a point of visibly referring to them (even if he really doesn't have to) to role model their use. In addition, leaders are proactive in monitoring their use and identifying any underlying causes where there is evidence of little use – e.g. flowchart of little relevance, hard to understand, difficult to access.

We regard key processes as vital in delivering the goals and objectives set out in our policy and strategy. To us, it is important to be able to constantly check the health of these key processes and test the degree to which they are delivering value to our stakeholders. Therefore, we have identified, at the highest level, our key process outcome measures, which relate both to satisfying customer as well as our own internal needs.

Process performance is reviewed at every monthly Board meeting, both in absolute terms and by evaluating performance against achievement of policy and strategy. Monthly reports to Board include those on Production Management, Quality and Health & Safety.

Links to Fundamental Concepts

- ☐ Leadership and constancy of purpose
- ☑ Management by process and facts
- ☐ People development and involvement
- ☐ Continuous learning, improvement and innovation
- ☐ Customer focus
- ☐ Partner development
- ☐ Public responsibility
- ☐ Results orientation

Links to Fundamental Concepts

- ☐ Leadership and constancy of purpose
- ☑ Management by process and facts
- ☐ People development and involvement
- ☐ Continuous learning, improvement and innovation
- ☐ Customer focus
- ☐ Partner development
- ☐ Public responsibility
- ☐ Results orientation

Criterion 5

3.5 Processes

How the organisation designs, manages and improves its processes in order to support its policy and strategy and fully satisfy, and generate increasing value for, its customers and other stakeholders.

Sub-criterion 5B:
Processes are improved, as needed, using innovation in order to fully satisfy and generate increasing value for customers and other stakeholders.

Areas to address may include:

- *Identifying and prioritising opportunities for improvement, and other changes, both incremental and breakthrough;*

- *Using performance and perception results and information from learning activities to set priorities and targets for improvement and improved methods of operation;*

- *Stimulating and bringing to bear the creative and innovative talents of employees, customers and partners in incremental and break through improvements;*

- *Discovering and using new process designs, operating philosophies and enabling technology;*

- *Establishing appropriate methods for implementing change;*

- *Piloting and controlling the implementation of new or changed processes;*

- *Communicating process changes to all appropriate stakeholders;*

- *Ensuring people are trained to operate new or changed processes prior to implementation;*

- *Ensuring process changes achieve predicted results.*

PRIVATE SECTOR

Employees from all levels are encouraged to improve and support their own and others' performance. One of the mediums through which this is possible is the Opportunities For Improvement system. Some opportunities for improvement result in the formation of a process group to assess and recommend/implement a solution. Usually, a process group is made up of staff from different departments. It always has a designated group leader and roles within the group are allocated as necessary depending on the needs of the group. Three examples of process improvement groups are, canteen improvement group, duty free goods-in group and export workflow improvement group. The results, which are agreed in the process group, are measured, where possible, using targets against budgets and monthly Key Process Indicators. The Opportunity For Improvement system is a powerful way in which all staff can suggest changes to the way the business is run and to improve their working environment in a constructive way.

Through performance management and the monthly monitoring of actual results against target, the Central Management Team, Depot Managers or staff, via line managers, can propose that a workshop is required. One example of this is a workshop held in October 2000 as a result of the People and Customer surveys. The Operations Manager and the Depot Manager selected attendees for the workshop. They were from all departments to give as wide a range of view as possible and to draw on different expertise. As a result of the workshop an action plan was implemented.

Links to Fundamental Concepts

☐ Leadership and constancy of purpose	☐ Customer focus
	☐ Partner development
☐ Management by process and facts	☐ Public responsibility
☑ People development and involvement	☐ Results orientation
☑ Continuous learning, improvement and innovation	

PUBLIC SECTOR

A small team incorporating external facilitators and Agency staff was established to undertake a major process review. The team systematically worked through a structured workshop approach with staff throughout the organisation. The essence of the review findings were a series of specific changes to processes that would eliminate non added value activities, improve efficiency in the delivery of added value and meet Services Modernisation aims agreed with the organisations main client.

The recommendations also highlighted the development of a team-based model, which was fundamental to the delivery of the changes. The team-based model is designed to:
• reduce compartmentalisation and maximising staff productivity
• provide a single, comprehensive team
• establish the Team Leader as process manager, work allocater, team builder and coach
• empower teams within a framework of clear operational policy
• increase the focus on quality assurance.

Opportunities were identified over the short, medium and longer term, which would greatly improve the financial benefits essential for re-investment into the organisation as well as to meet immediate business pressures. Other benefits were identified from the potential impact of legislative change and wider organisational opportunities.

From the outset a communication strategy was built on openness and understanding of key business issues and led by senior managers. Ongoing process change is being communicated through comprehensive use of the organisations Intranet and a programme of workshops with key managers, team leaders and staff.

Links to Fundamental Concepts

☐ Leadership and constancy of purpose
☑ Management by process and facts
☑ People development and involvement
☑ Continuous learning, improvement and innovation
☐ Customer focus
☐ Partner development
☐ Public responsibility
☐ Results orientation

SMALL/MEDIUM

At the Strategic Review each January all key processes are reviewed for effectiveness by the Executive Team/Management Team. This identifies achievements already made and identifies weaknesses that will provide opportunities for improvements. The Executive Team/Management Team use a consensus based approach for prioritising these improvements and for selecting a member of the team to take responsibility for researching and implementing the improvements. Priorities are set according to how quickly an improvement has to be implemented and are also dependent on the size of the improvement and the expected benefit to the business.

Incremental improvements are implemented through the day-to-day running of the business and can effectively be managed on an individual or team basis. Breakthrough improvements are identified as those which will have a major impact on the success of the business. Responsibility for breakthrough improvements is allocated to one member of the Executive Team/Management Team who will see the improvement through to full implementation but will call on the resources of other members of the team when required.

The creative talents of employees, customers and partners are used in making process improvements within the company. Breakthrough improvements include the Managing Director having to develop the processes for the implementation of the Quality Management System and the Human Resource Development developing improved Human Resource management processes in the drive for Investors in People certification as a result of our management consultants introducing us to Investors in People in 1996. Incremental improvements resulting from employees creative talents include an operative suggesting a change to the way the schedules have been set up to create more relevant and timely information.

Links to Fundamental Concepts

☐ Leadership and constancy of purpose
☑ Management by process and facts
☑ People development and involvement
☑ Continuous learning, improvement and innovation
☐ Customer focus
☐ Partner development
☐ Public responsibility
☐ Results orientation

3.5 | Processes

How the organisation designs, manages and improves its processes in order to support its policy and strategy and fully satisfy, and generate increasing value for, its customers and other stakeholders.

Sub-criterion 5C:
Products and services are designed and developed based on customer needs and expectations.

Areas to address may include:

- *Using market research, customer surveys and other forms of feedback to determine customer needs and expectations for products and services both now and in the future, and their perceptions of existing products and services;*

- *Anticipating and identifying improvements aimed at enhancing products and services in line with customers' future needs and expectations;*

- *Designing and developing new products and services to address the needs and expectations of customers;*

- *Using creativity and innovation to develop competitive products and services;*

- *Generating new products with partners.*

PRIVATE SECTOR

We have a formal product development and review process linked in to our annual planning process and based on extensive customer research. There is continuous review of customer views and opinions by means of formal, informal, direct and indirect research. This evidence, together with other information on business environment, political, economic and environmental developments is used by product development teams to design new products and assess existing product performance.

People are encouraged to recognise the benefits of treating colleagues and other departments as their customer and applying the same processes to deliver satisfaction that is applied to external customers. The approach is about basing business decisions upon customer's needs to achieve targeted objectives.

We use research programmes, customer visits and focus groups to identify customer needs and encourage suggestions for future developments and tracking, service standards and competitor monitoring. Research findings have also contributed to the formulation of policy including a move to instalment payments, discount schemes, re-scoping, colour advertising and new products such as new Business Page Directories.

New research studies include reviews of multi-product purchase customers, a review of the Financial Services market and testing of options on pricing packages.

Links to Fundamental Concepts

☐ Leadership and constancy of purpose	☑ Customer focus
	☐ Partner development
☑ Management by process and facts	☐ Public responsibility
☐ People development and involvement	☐ Results orientation
☐ Continuous learning, improvement and innovation	

Criterion 5

PUBLIC SECTOR The most important part of our business is tenant involvement. Put simply, tenant involvement means giving tenants control over all decisions that affect the way their homes are managed.

In 1999 the Housing Corporation gave the Housing Trust an innovation and good practice grant of £20,000 to publish a guide to customer feedback for other Trusts. The Corporation supported this project in recognition of the reputation we have in the sector.

In 1995 the Group appointed a quality manager to take forward our commitment to quality services, quality homes. The quality manager developed a range of techniques and methods for assessing customer views including the use of telephone surveys, reception surveys, focus groups and monitoring of satisfaction with the repairs service.

In 1996 we launched the customer service guarantee, which all parts of the Group have now adopted. The guarantee was an innovation in the sector, setting out in black and white the standard of service tenants could expect from whichever part of the Group they came into contact with If we fall short of the service we have a system of giving customer service payments and gifts.

The quality manager role was broadened to a corporate position in 1999 with the specific brief of championing customer care and designing feedback and learning systems in all parts of the Group.

We recognise that it is the day-to-day contact that tenants have with us that determines their perceptions. Every contact is a "moment of truth" and can build positive or negative impressions.

Each moment of truth therefore is a test of the relevance of policy and strategy and the effectiveness of our processes.

SMALL/MEDIUM Various feedback mechanisms are employed to ensure that we are alert to any change in customer perceptions.

There are strong process elements involved in important customer based activities such as complaints and in ordering procedures and product queries. Staff are constantly reminded how easy it is to upset customers.

The contact and marketing database has been carefully and methodically improved and, with a good deal of input from many sources, brought up to date. The list was reduced from 1250 to 800 potential laboratories with a further breakdown by several measures. This has made targeting prospects for new products much more effective, e.g. English mail shot for Progressions had a 27% response rate, the French 47%, the Spanish 17% and Italian 12.5%.

Other areas of marketing activity have been addressed and are a vital part of the processes of the company. All brochures and leaflets are password protected and are voluntary part of the ISO 9001 system. A market intelligence process is in operation, which gives an overview of developments and the potential buy out of an UK competitor by a US competitor was isolated by this data.

Both the complaints system and customer surveys showed that products stability had been a problem area and, following an analysis of this data we introduced two new products and positive customer feedback to these launches was reflected in subsequent surveys and complaints levels. Similarly, customer survey response was used to test market reaction to the launch of one of our new products and we used a dedicated mail-shot survey with telephone follow up to secure accurate feedback.

Mere incremental product improvements often based on anecdotal evidence or perceptions are cited by competitors and this often clouds the customer's true perceptions.

Links to Fundamental Concepts

☐ Leadership and constancy of purpose
☑ Management by process and facts
☐ People development and involvement
☐ Continuous learning, improvement and innovation
☑ Customer focus
☐ Partner development
☐ Public responsibility
☐ Results orientation

Links to Fundamental Concepts

☐ Leadership and constancy of purpose
☑ Management by process and facts
☐ People development and involvement
☐ Continuous learning, improvement and innovation
☑ Customer focus
☐ Partner development
☐ Public responsibility
☐ Results orientation

Criterion 5

3.5 Processes

How the organisation designs, manages and improves its processes in order to support its policy and strategy and fully satisfy, and generate increasing value for, its customers and other stakeholders.

Sub-criterion 5D:
Products and services are produced, delivered and serviced.

Areas to address may include:

- *Producing or acquiring products and services in line with designs and developments;*

- *Communicating, marketing and selling products and services to existing and potential customers;*

- *Delivering products and services to customers;*

- *Servicing products and services, where appropriate.*

PRIVATE SECTOR

The physical way in which we communicate our products and services to customers is at the forefront of technology. We use the latest presentational software packages which even allow us to include full video clips of adverts to be shown on a laptop or via an LCD projector, all of which has made us more efficient and builds a professional image.

Following a review of our operating processes with design agencies, to speed our ability to approve (or reject) designs from agencies, we have developed a system whereby electronic 'Post-it' notes can be attached to a design on-screen which is then returned to the agency without having to be printed. This will reduce the time to produce final visuals of new products and packaging/ Point of Sale material.

Following the introduction and a review of our ERP application it was identified that we were unable at the time to support a stock allocation system. This meant that when a product was selling faster than expected and using higher volume than forecast for one account, stock for other accounts was being used to fulfil orders. As we produce stock to forecast this would lead to us running low or out of stock, being unable to deliver to other accounts. The ERP application has now been developed to able to allocate stock for delivery by account. This has increased the level of 'Delivered in Full' deliveries and ensured there is emphasis on the forecasting by account.

Other new processes from these reviews include: capped volume, which sets the upper limits of volume for a customer for a promotional pack and Agreed Buy In Dates which sets the precise timings for customers talking stock. This ensures a smooth flow from the production stage through to delivery. Looking further ahead, the changing retailing market place will impact us at every level. 24 hour lead times, seven days operations and co-managed ordering and inventories are just some of the many things altering our way of working.

Links to Fundamental Concepts

☐ Leadership and constancy of purpose

☑ Customer focus

☑ Management by process and facts

☐ Partner development

☐ Public responsibility

☐ People development and involvement

☐ Results orientation

☑ Continuous learning, improvement and innovation

PUBLIC SECTOR

Values of professionalism and customer focus. This is supported by the use of class management files (Red and Blue files). These promote individual reflection on practice which are subsequently reviewed by the Head or Deputy twice a term. They are discussed as part of the Staff Development Interview procedure and by an active encouragement and sharing of customer and supplier feedback, e.g. school inspection reports, survey reports and the minutes of meetings.

Steps have also been taken over the years to increase the level of empowerment of non-teaching staff. Examples would be the transfer of duties from teachers to other members of staff and the increasing involvement of nursery nurses in school development planning which started in the mid 80s. The ongoing emphasis on communication, active involvement and participation results in many creative improvement suggestions which often can be funded from school funds and which have a small but significant impact on the service provided.

Major process changes usually involve the designation of a project leader with the responsibility to investigate current practice, make specific recommendations for action, and co-ordinate implementation. Projects of this type may be triggered by a need identified by the Senior Management team or in response to specific proposals bids made by staff.

SMALL/MEDIUM

Products and services are produced, delivered and serviced by: Communicating, marketing and selling services to existing and potential customers; delivering quality services to customers.

The College is on the cutting edge developing curriculum within the vocational area with its development of online products. With its development of a new Federation and Academy is implementing future policies set out by the previous green paper. The College has effective communication, marketing, selling and delivery processes, this is demonstrated very strongly by the over subscription of the College; the creation of the proliferation of multimedia productions.

There are several teams who are working on future developments especially with intranet communications that gives a vast network of communication systems to both customers and suppliers. There is comprehensive evidence of a well-managed process, which ensures the delivery of quality teaching and that the superb outcomes can be measured. The process management set out by the management gives clear evidence that the College has effective processes that ensure relevant programmes, products and services are delivered to the appropriate stakeholder groups.

Links to Fundamental Concepts

- ☐ Leadership and constancy of purpose
- ☑ Customer focus
- ☑ Management by process and facts
- ☐ Partner development
- ☐ People development and involvement
- ☐ Public responsibility
- ☐ Results orientation
- ☐ Continuous learning, improvement and innovation

Links to Fundamental Concepts

- ☐ Leadership and constancy of purpose
- ☑ Customer focus
- ☑ Management by process and facts
- ☐ Partner development
- ☐ People development and involvement
- ☐ Public responsibility
- ☐ Results orientation
- ☐ Continuous learning, improvement and innovation

Criterion 5

3.5 | Processes

How the organisation designs, manages and improves its processes in order to support its policy and strategy and fully satisfy, and generate increasing value for, its customers and other stakeholders.

Sub-criterion 5E:
Customer relationships are managed and enhanced.

Areas to address may include:

- *Determining and meeting customers' day-to-day contact requirements;*

- *Handling feedback received from day-to-day contacts including complaints;*

- *Proactive involvement with customers to discuss and address their needs, expectations and concerns;*

- *Following up on sales, servicing and other contacts to determine levels of satisfaction with products, services and other customer sales and servicing processes;*

- *Seeking to maintain creativity and innovation in the customer sales and servicing relationship;*

- *Using regular surveys, other forms of structured data gathering and data gathered during day-to-day customer contacts in order to determine and enhance customer relationship satisfaction levels.*

PRIVATE SECTOR

There are strong process elements involved in important customer based activities such as complaints and in ordering procedures and product queries.

The contract and marketing database has been carefully and methodically improved and, with a good deal of input from many sources, brought up to date.

All operating companies undertake market research at least once a year in advance of and integrated with the business planning process. This assists in identifying and qualifying the care requirements of customers and consumers. The research must ascertain the importance to the customer of the care criteria. Action plans are compiled based on the findings.

All operating companies monitor and report customer/ client satisfaction at least once a year. The survey must measure the level of satisfaction achieved for various specific criteria. At unit level, each unit will use either suggestion box/book or customer comment cards to monitor feedback. Any complaints are documented and action plans compiled based on trends. Every attempt is made to speak to customers, both direct and further along the supply chain, to ascertain their requirements for new developments and products.

The sales force is briefed to ask relevant questions about products and services and feed this information back.

Links to Fundamental Concepts

☐ Leadership and constancy of purpose

☐ Management by process and facts

☐ People development and involvement

☐ Continuous learning, improvement and innovation

☑ Customer focus

☐ Partner development

☐ Public responsibility

☐ Results orientation

PUBLIC SECTOR

Through tenant involvement, the relationship between client and customer is improved. Tenants are both clients and customers and are involved at all levels of the business. The ways in which tenants can be directly involved has been developed to be as flexible as possible. This gives people a choice of how much involvement they want and at the level that suits them. Tenants can set policy, strategy, budgets, timetables and priorities.

Area committees set their own budgets and oversee the management of the local area. The area committees are written into many housing, management and reinvestment processes, which ensures that their members have real influence over what happens locally. Area committees also have a key role in our performance management system. Local performance indicators are reported quarterly to the area committee. In addition to monitoring performance, area committees agree which indicators of performance they wish to see.

At a local level tenants are encouraged to form tenants associations. Customer service managers meet the tenant association monthly. Tenants associations decide what issues have priority locally through estate agreements. Members of the tenants association oversee progress against the agreement and local customer service managers are accountable to them. The agreement has been delivered to every tenant on the estate and gives added kudos to the residents association. The agreement recognises the role and importance of tenant involvement and participation.

SMALL/MEDIUM

Since its inception, the trust has sought to develop a careers management process and a comprehensive support infrastructure designed to meet the needs of a unique client base: serving and former members of the Royal Ulster Constabulary and the Royal Ulster Constabulary Full Time Reserve. The trust has assisted more than 1500 former and serving police officers, including 700 members of the Full Time Reserve during the past 2 years.

Comprehensive training is presented in all identified areas of need. A careers support system has also similarly developed to include a discretionary training/education grant scheme, established working relationships with key employers, recruitment agencies, universities and training colleges, and over 25 consultant professionals in various disciplines who offer tuition, mentoring and coaching to our clients. In addition a newly developed careers workbook underpins the careers management process, further enabling the Trust's clients to take direct and continuing control of their own career choices.

For those officers who cannot visit the Trust because of injury or incapacity, comprehensive coaching and mentoring services are provided at home in subject areas such as CV, business finance and marketing, franchising, study techniques, and mathematics.

Appropriate referral to our psychological or physiotherapy services also provides a truly seamless and holistic service to all of our clients. This service will continue to be available to all members of the Full Time Reserve as part of the overall provision and enhancement of services during the Outplacement Programme.

Links to Fundamental Concepts

- ☐ Leadership and constancy of purpose
- ☑ Management by process and facts
- ☐ People development and involvement
- ☐ Continuous learning, improvement and innovation
- ☑ Customer focus
- ☐ Partner development
- ☐ Public responsibility
- ☐ Results orientation

Links to Fundamental Concepts

- ☐ Leadership and constancy of purpose
- ☑ Management by process and facts
- ☐ People development and involvement
- ☐ Continuous learning, improvement and innovation
- ☑ Customer focus
- ☐ Partner development
- ☐ Public responsibility
- ☐ Results orientation

Criterion 5

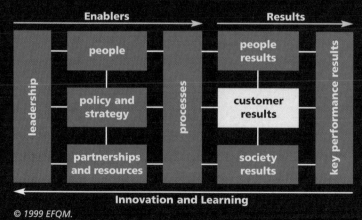

The Excellence Model

Enablers → Results →

leadership | people | processes | people results | key performance results
policy and strategy | | customer results |
partnerships and resources | | society results |

← Innovation and Learning

© 1999 EFQM.

The organisation's achievements with respect to its customers, based on their opinions and the organisation's measures.

2A Establishing customers' needs and expectations

2C Balancing customers' needs and expectations

1C Leaders' involvement with customers

1 Leadership

2 Policy and Strategy

6 Customer Results

5 Processes

3 People

5B Improving processes to satisfy customers

5C Product and service development

5D Product and service delivery

5E Customer relationship management

4 Partnerships and Resources

4A Good supplier/partner relationships to satisfy customers

3B People have the skills and competencies to deal with customers

3C People's involvement with customers

Linkages with the enablers

3.6 Customer Results

W hat the organisation is achieving in relation to its external customers.

Sub-criterion 6A:
Perception measures.

Areas to address may include:

- *Overall image – accessibility, communication, flexibility, proactive behaviour, responsiveness;*

- *Products and services – quality, value, reliability, design innovation, delivery, environmental profile;*

- *Sales and after-sales support – capabilities and behaviour of employees, advice and support, customer literature and technical documentation, handling complaints, product training, response time, technical support, warranty and guarantee provisions;*

- *Loyalty – intention to repurchase, willingness to purchase other products and services from the organisation, willingness to recommend the organisation.*

PRIVATE SECTOR

Our commitment and dedication to customer satisfaction is not only reflected in the Division's objectives, but in the results of the customer satisfaction surveys. Performance is measured against these results on an ongoing basis and stratagem adopted to improve the perception of our customers. We are looking for year on year improvements in all areas, and target specific areas of concerns – e.g. Customer Satisfaction Survey 2001, Teleorder identified accuracy levels, stock availability, and making customers feel valued. A brainstorming session subsequently came up with an action plan for improving customer perception in these areas, we look forward to the 2002 survey to see how successful we have been. Because this Customer Satisfaction Survey is specific to our client organisation we have recently formed a relationship with a local company. This will enable us to benchmark and share best practice with a similar business to our own, we believe it will be a useful union in the future.

We also measure customer satisfaction through our customer loyalty and willingness to expand the scope of our business dealing. Over the time we have been dealing with our client organisation the majority of units think the service offered has improved, and performance against targets in most areas has shown a year on year improvement.

Links to Fundamental Concepts

- ☐ Leadership and constancy of purpose
- ☑ Management by process and facts
- ☐ People development and involvement
- ☐ Continuous learning, improvement and innovation
- ☑ Customer focus
- ☐ Partner development
- ☐ Public responsibility
- ☐ Results orientation

criterion 6

PUBLIC SECTOR

Our Customer First Strategy was launched in 1996 and is being reviewed. The current survey is used to gather customer perceptions of the services we provide and includes a section asking customers if these aspects of service are still relevant and important. Feedback is then fed into any review of the survey.

Our customer surveys ask our customers to rank how well we perform each of the aspects of service using a scale of one to three. The surveys also ask customers to list two or three things we do particularly well as well as any service provision improvements or opportunities the customer feels could be examined. The Customer Satisfaction Index is a measure we identified during the Service Study Benchmarking exercise. The Customer Satisfaction Index is the percentage of our customers who rank our overall level of a particular service to them as acceptable or better. The Service Study exercise identified a Customer Service Index of 75% as placing us in the top quartile of organisations using the study in terms of customer satisfaction. The change in our survey (moving from a score between one and four to a clearer system involving only three alternative scores) has produced a quantum step in terms of our scores. Comparators in this area are hard to establish as definitions of satisfaction differ between organisations.

The European Quality Award winner for 2000 includes the following benchmarks for correspondence surveys; 1999 EQA 87%, 1999 Public Sector Benchmarks 82% and 88% and 1999 Departmental Survey 82%. Our score of 85% compares well with these figures.

SMALL/MEDIUM

In 1996 Priority Search carried out a sample survey of our tenants. Respondents were asked to select the top ten services or facilities that they regarded as the most important. Repairs are clearly the most important cited by 80% of respondents, followed by security improvements and home improvements. The first six of these, areas have all been subject to a project approach to improvement.

Our tenants tell us this is the most important aspect of the service we provide. The main pieces of research conducted into repairs have been the 1987 Mori survey and, starting in 1995, our regular 1 in 3 repairs satisfaction survey carried out by Priority Search. We should point out that we actually suspended this programme of research in November 1998, based on the belief that we were not achieving value for money from the research contractors, that limited information was being generated, and that the quality and focus of work had not been formally evaluated. We did ensure that we included questions on our repairs service in the March 1999 Tenants Survey to ensure that we did not lose valuable performance data on the service, and are currently exploring different ways of gathering future feedback from our tenants in line with the Research Strategy.

In 1987, 78% of respondents were very or fairly satisfied by the service provided. Following our 'Ordering a day-to-day repair' first generation quality project, we started the measurements shown above. Since then we have maintained and improved upon consistently high levels of satisfaction with 80%–90% consistently agreeing with the statement "the staff were helpful when I reported the repair".

Links to Fundamental Concepts

☐ Leadership and constancy of purpose
☑ Management by process and facts
☐ People development and involvement
☐ Continuous learning, improvement and innovation
☑ Customer focus
☐ Partner development
☐ Public responsibility
☐ Results orientation

Links to Fundamental Concepts

☐ Leadership and constancy of purpose
☑ Management by process and facts
☐ People development and involvement
☐ Continuous learning, improvement and innovation
☑ Customer focus
☐ Partner development
☐ Public responsibility
☐ Results orientation

Criterion 6

3.6 | Customer Results

What the organisation is achieving in relation to its external customers.

Sub-criterion 6B:
Performance indicators.

Areas to address may include:

- *Overall image – number of customer accolades and nominations for awards, press coverage;*

- *Products and services – competitiveness, defect, error and rejection rates, guarantee provisions and warranty provisions, complaints, logistic indicators, product life cycle, innovation in design, time to market;*

- *Sales and after-sales support – demand for training, handling of complaints, response rates;*

- *Loyalty – duration of relationship, effective recommendations, frequency/value of orders, lifetime value, number of complaints and compliments, new and/or lost business, customer retention.*

 PRIVATE SECTOR We have a range of measures we use to predict the level of satisfaction of our customers. The core ones are:

Yield Premium: Whilst a financial business result, this figure is seen across the industry as a key measure of the satisfaction of customers.

Complaints and Compliments: Whilst all the establishments own and manage their complaints and compliments themselves, we also consider trends centrally to identify corporate issues based on complaints received. We measure both the absolute number of complaints as well as the ratio between rooms sold and complaints. The results show that the crucial figure of complaints is coming down. We are still in the process of establishing the culture of tracking and sharing the compliments beyond the hotel associates.

Sales: Clearly sales figures are an indicator of customer satisfaction. Our sales figures show an improving year on year performance.

Market Share: Market share in the hotel business is measured in number of rooms available and can be increased whether customers are satisfied with the hotel's performance or not. For this reason we do not perceive this to be a predicator of customer satisfaction. We do however consider "brand market share" to be important. This is based on customer recall of brands used in the last year and is tracked independently. Our current position is 5.7%, which compares favourably with our competition.

Membership: Membership numbers for our golf and leisure clubs are clearly a predictor of customer loyalty. Our total membership has grown year on year for both leisure and golf despite the increasing competition across the market.

Links to Fundamental Concepts

- ☐ Leadership and constancy of purpose
- ☑ Management by process and facts
- ☐ People development and involvement
- ☐ Continuous learning, improvement and innovation
- ☑ Customer focus
- ☐ Partner development
- ☐ Public responsibility
- ☐ Results orientation

PUBLIC SECTOR

Our performance indicators for customer satisfaction are based on the standards of the customer service Guarantee. The measures in the guarantee were devised as part of the housing, services review in 1995. This year we have consulted with tenants to update and improve the measures to focus them more clearly on current tenant expectations. In addition to the guarantee we set ourselves targets around aspects of the maintenance service that tenants have told us are important to them. These published standards set the performance indicators that are used in the service departments, housing, services and property services. Performance is reported to our director of housing and our property services director and then in turn to the area committees and the Board.

The standard across the Group is to answer phones within 5 rings. We use our telephony systems to measure the length of time people have to wait before a call is picked up. On average we answer calls in less than 3 rings and have been consistently meeting, the standard since it was set in 1996, despite increasing telephone contact with our tenants.

We set two targets, one to acknowledge all correspondence within 3 working days, the other to respond to all letters within 10 days. We have developed an in-house tracking, system to keep tabs on all letters and have appointed 'letter loggers' in each office, who chase staff when responses are due. Our rates of acknowledgement are extremely good and are improving, year by year towards our target.

SMALL/MEDIUM

OFSTED, in March 1994, found that "This is a good college. As a result of high motivation and sound teaching, the standards achieved by the students are good or better." In November 1997 OFSTED stated, the College is providing a very good education with some excellent features. As well as enabling its students to achieve very well academically, it successfully encourages their personal development through a very wide range of opportunities within and beyond the College. The College provides good value for money. The College had no key issues for action; this is very rare with one other school now achieving this. The College's success is also unequivocally demonstrated in its yearly applications for places and high student attendance. This is an indication that the processes applied are clearly meeting the needs of our customers.

The College has been further endorsed by DfEE and Government through its successful application to be the first private company to take over a failing school.

An outstanding school in the Inspectors Report and was invited to apply for training school status which it has just won. The College has also received very prestigious awards, including the TNT Modernising Government Partnership Award, the Schools Curriculum Award. Investor in People, also awarded to the College, is the quality benchmark that allows all types of organisations to be recognised for investment in human resources – more tangible evidence of satisfaction by the awarding bodies.

A major student need is to gain recognised qualifications; the College succeeds exceptionally well and when Key Stage 4 results are compared with national averages the College results are double the national results. When compared to a neighbouring school in the same catchment area drawing on similar students the College is scoring 65% better.

Links to Fundamental Concepts

- ☐ Leadership and constancy of purpose
- ☑ Management by process and facts
- ☐ People development and involvement
- ☐ Continuous learning, improvement and innovation
- ☑ Customer focus
- ☐ Partner development
- ☐ Public responsibility
- ☐ Results orientation

Links to Fundamental Concepts

- ☐ Leadership and constancy of purpose
- ☑ Management by process and facts
- ☐ People development and involvement
- ☐ Continuous learning, improvement and innovation
- ☑ Customer focus
- ☐ Partner development
- ☐ Public responsibility
- ☐ Results orientation

Criterion 6

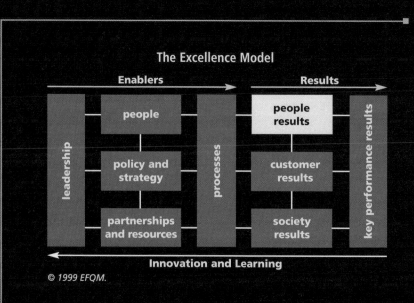

The Excellence Model

Enablers → Results →

leadership

people

policy and strategy

partnerships and resources

processes

people results

customer results

society results

key performance results

← Innovation and Learning

© 1999 EFQM.

"The organisation's achievements with respect to its employees, based on their opinions and the organisation's measures."

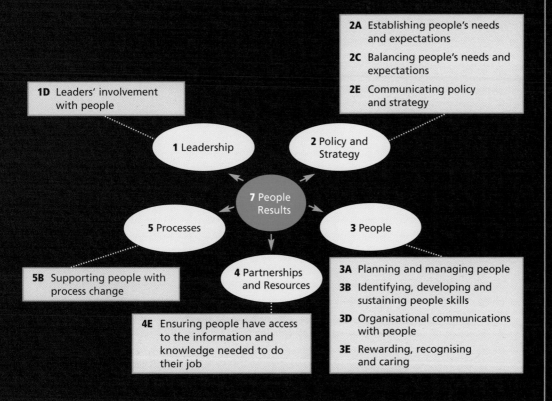

2A Establishing people's needs and expectations

2C Balancing people's needs and expectations

2E Communicating policy and strategy

1D Leaders' involvement with people

1 Leadership

2 Policy and Strategy

7 People Results

5 Processes

3 People

5B Supporting people with process change

4 Partnerships and Resources

3A Planning and managing people

3B Identifying, developing and sustaining people skills

3D Organisational communications with people

3E Rewarding, recognising and caring

4E Ensuring people have access to the information and knowledge needed to do their job

Linkages with the enablers

3.7 | People Results

What the organisation is achieving in relation to its people.

Sub-criterion 7A:
Perception measures.

Areas to address may include:

- *Motivation – career development, communication, empowerment, equal opportunities, involvement, leadership, opportunity to learn and achieve, recognition, target setting and appraisal, the organisation's values, vision, mission, policy and strategy, training and development;*

- *Satisfaction – organisation's administration, employment conditions, facilities and services, health and safety conditions, job security, pay and benefits, peer relationships, the management of change, the organisation's environmental policy and impact, the organisation's role in the community and society, working environment.*

PRIVATE SECTOR We recognise the importance of our people in delivering the level of service that will keep our Guests satisfied and generate the loyalty that will enable us to achieve the financial performance expected by our operational stakeholder. This belief is embedded in our Vision.

To enable us to formally track the satisfaction and motivation of our associate we use two key surveys, the Associate Opinion Survey and the Views survey. The Associate Opinion Survey provides detailed information on the levels of satisfaction of associates. It has been developed based on the important issues identified through focus groups with associates and is reviewed annually on the basis of these inputs. The survey consists of over 50 questions covering a wide range of issues including:
- senior management performance
- the job and tools for the job
- pay and conditions
- fairness of policies
- opportunity for advancement
- training and induction
- dealing with customers
- cross-functional working.

As part of our balanced scorecard we have set increasingly stretching targets for these two questions. In 1997 we were trying to achieve a 79% satisfaction level overall this rose to 81% in 1998, 82% in 1999 and is targeted at 84% in 2000 and 85% in 2001. The above results show we have achieved close to or above target levels every year. In addition to these targets the units will focus themselves on particular questions, which are relevant to their own circumstances and prepare targets for these measures.

Links to Fundamental Concepts

☐ Leadership and constancy of purpose

☑ Management by process and facts

☑ People development and involvement

☐ Continuous learning, improvement and innovation

☐ Customer focus

☐ Partner development

☐ Public responsibility

☐ Results orientation

Criterion 7

PUBLIC SECTOR From 1987 to 1994 we measured people satisfaction through a series of attitude surveys, annual focus group meetings and road shows. In 1994 we adopted the EFQM Excellence Model as our main driver for achieving business excellence and since then we have carried out annual surveys to chart our progress and inform our Strategic Planning Process.

Our annual employee satisfaction survey is aligned to the criteria of the EFQM Excellence Model and is reviewed annually. New survey questionnaires are successfully piloted before being implemented.

All 1000 plus employees take part in our survey each year. Our current questionnaire asks 44 questions on all factors relating, to employee satisfaction and motivation. The questionnaire is anonymous. Results are segmented and analysed by Business Unit and Pay Band. The results form the basis of action plans that address areas for improvement.

Our results show sustained high performance with favourable satisfaction levels of over 70%, with many of the results over 90% for the last 3 years. Benchmarking information shows many of our results to be World Class.

Our aim is to maintain our consistently high performance with a minimum overall tolerance of 80% satisfaction.

Our people satisfaction indicator is used to measure overall progress to enable comparisons between different Business Units and to identify trends in people satisfaction levels. This is based on the number of favourable and unfavourable responses and expressed as a score out of 10.

Our 1999 target is to achieve at least seven out of 10. Equal Opportunity issues are key features of our Caring, for Staff Strategies. Everyone has received training in Equal Opportunities. In 1997 and 1998 over 99% of our people were aware of the Agency Equal Opportunity policy.

SMALL/MEDIUM In 1996, we conducted a staff survey within the Housing Services department (120 staff), and in 1998 piloted a staff survey using a different technique on 25% of staff. Although we were gathering some information, we knew that this was an area we needed to improve on.

In March 1999, we commissioned an independent Research company to conduct a full staff satisfaction survey that generated a 53% response rate. This is the first of an annual programme. The questionnaire used was built following meetings with those involved in Social Audit and IIP, managers and 35 randomly selected staff in four focus groups. Due to the different approaches taken in these surveys we are unable to directly compare results. However in the future we will be studying trends.

Generally, this area rated positively. When staff were asked how they felt about customer service generally within, 54% said they thought it was improving.

The most positively rated statements related to team communication. 75% of respondents are aware of the Trust's Mission and Values. The management style results are encouraging, with generally line managers viewed with respect and as good leaders. When asked to positively rate management styles, the most highly rated were Honest, Approachable, Listener, Supportive and Customer focused. There were highest ratings for the statement of challenging procedures, being supported by line manager and encouraged to put forward new ideas.

Training and development generally received a positive rating. The most positively rated statements are in the area of working environment and job security.

Links to Fundamental Concepts

☐ Leadership and constancy of purpose
☐ Customer focus
☐ Partner development
☑ Management by process and facts
☐ Public responsibility
☑ People development and involvement
☐ Results orientation
☐ Continuous learning, improvement and innovation

Links to Fundamental Concepts

☐ Leadership and constancy of purpose
☐ Customer focus
☐ Partner development
☑ Management by process and facts
☐ Public responsibility
☑ People development and involvement
☐ Results orientation
☐ Continuous learning, improvement and innovation

Criterion 7

3.7 | People Results

hat the organisation is achieving in relation to its people.

Sub-criterion 7B:
Performance indicators.

Areas to address may include:

- *Achievements – competency requirements versus competencies available, productivity, success rates of training and development to meet objectives;*

- *Motivation and involvement – involvement in improvement teams, involvement in suggestion schemes, levels of training and development, measurable benefits of teamwork, recognition of individuals and teams, response rates to people surveys;*

- *Satisfaction – absenteeism and sickness levels, accident levels, grievances, recruitment trends, staff turnover, strikes, use of benefits, use of organisation provided facilities, (e.g. recreational, crèche);*

- *Services provided to the organisation's people – accuracy of personnel administration, communication effectiveness, speed of response to enquiries, training evaluation.*

PRIVATE SECTOR

Given the importance we place on our staff, we recognise the need to be able to manage associate satisfaction and motivation based on information that can be captured more frequently than the "perception measures". In the Hotel and Leisure industry the primary predictor of the satisfaction and motivation of staff is your ability to keep staff. Average turnover in the industry is currently running at between 70% and 80%. The best of our competitors have turnover rates in excess of 50%. This is such an important measure that it constitutes one of our "top line" measures in our balanced scorecard. Our results show our performance is amongst the best in the industry.

Response rates on the survey have risen from 80% to 85% to 86% year on year. Given this is a voluntary survey the extremely high response rate clearly demonstrates a commitment. Our commitment to our staff includes helping them to develop their careers therefore we set a target to fill 75% of vacancies through internal appointment. This target was achieved.

The desire of our people to get involved in the business is demonstrated through the success of the 'Tell Alan' process. We have received 703 suggestions in the last year, 47% of these are either addressed or in the process of implementation or under review.

Links to Fundamental Concepts

- ☐ Leadership and constancy of purpose
- ☑ Management by process and facts
- ☑ People development and involvement
- ☐ Continuous learning, improvement and innovation
- ☐ Customer focus
- ☐ Partner development
- ☐ Public responsibility
- ☐ Results orientation

Criterion 7

Our response rate for the National Survey consistently exceeds the national rate. Our Regional Survey was a 100% census with 67% responding.

Equal Opportunities: We perform well against the national average for employing women in management grades, particularly at the most senior levels.

Employee Benefits: This expenditure includes nursery care and special aids for people with disabilities, which have increased significantly year on year since 1996/7.

Benevolent Fund: The Benevolent Fund is the last remaining Independent benevolent fund in the public sector. It assists staff in financial need. The increase in expenditure during 1999 is a result of our Fund Committee carrying out activities to market awareness of the fund plus an increase in amounts being awarded.

Our Resource Director has discretion to award Special Bonuses to individuals or teams who have demonstrated outstanding performance.

We continue to address attendance management through our People Strategy and can show fewer working days lost than all other regions with a consequent downward trend and improvement against the national average. In the last year 148 vacancies in the region have been filled by upward progression. This represents around 6% of our people.

We have 203 qualified National Vocational Qualification assessors and 117 working towards the award. 138 of our people hold National Vocational Qualification Level 3 in Customer Service and 34 are working towards it.

We are one of only four regions to achieve the national target for 90% to achieve Level 3 in Guidance by March 2000.

Links to Fundamental Concepts

☐ Leadership and constancy of purpose
☐ Customer focus
☐ Partner development
☑ Management by process and facts
☐ Public responsibility
☐ Results orientation
☑ People development and involvement
☐ Continuous learning, improvement and innovation

The Investors in People Award was granted in February 1995, reassessed in 1998 and 2001 to reflect the changed indicators. The Investor in People standard demands that all staff be aware of the College goals and how training and development will be geared to help them achieve their objectives. The College complies with the standard and the staff are aware of how they can contribute to the success of the College.

Employee Surveys demonstrate the success of the College's internal policies in developing its staff and were taken at the annual conference. On Professional Development Satisfaction, 91% of employees said they were very satisfied. This is compared to a norm of 57% for the area in which the CTC is, which gives the CTC a 34% difference over the local target rate.

Involvement, training and a hands-on approach to improvement have contributed to the responses from staff. The Governors, Principal and Management Team undertake to maintain and improve training activities for staff that is supported by the appraisals and target setting system. In addition, there is a signed statement from the Principal and the Chair of Governors that reinforces the backing of the Governors and Management Team towards the principle of commitment.

Area Managers evaluate development actions from reports received from individuals. Appraisal gives individuals the opportunity to reflect upon positive and negative training experiences against their own individual objectives, which in the majority of case are directly linked to the business objectives of the College Development Plan. In addition, members of staff who have attended external courses are invited to share their evaluation of the course with other members of staff at special sessions at the annual training conference.

Links to Fundamental Concepts

☐ Leadership and constancy of purpose
☐ Customer focus
☐ Partner development
☑ Management by process and facts
☐ Public responsibility
☐ Results orientation
☑ People development and involvement
☐ Continuous learning, improvement and innovation

Criterion 7

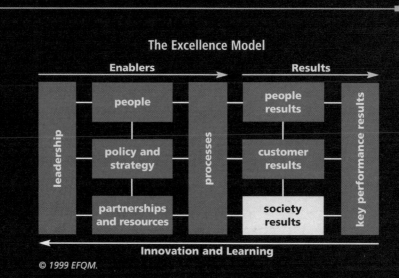

The Excellence Model

Enablers   Results

leadership

people   people
                                results

policy and   customer
strategy   processes   results   key performance results

partnerships   society
and resources   results

Innovation and Learning

© 1999 EFQM.

*"The organisation's
achievements with
respect to society
and the local
community, based
on their opinions
and the
organisation's
measures."*

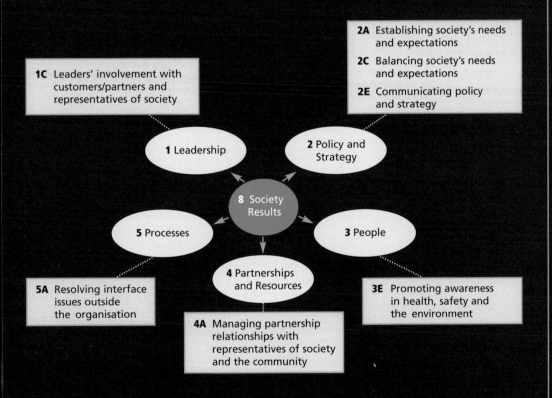

Linkages with
the enablers

3.8 Society Results

What the organisation is achieving in relation to local, national and international society as appropriate.

Sub-criterion 8A:
Perception measures.

Areas to address may include:

- *Performance as a responsible citizen – disclosures of information relevant to the community, equal opportunities practices, impact on local and national economies, relationships with relevant authorities, ethical behaviour;*

- *Involvement in the communities where it operates – involvement in education and training, support for medical and welfare provision, support for sport and leisure, voluntary work and philanthropy;*

- *Activities to reduce and prevent nuisance and harm from its operations and/or throughout the life cycle of its products – health risks and accidents, noise and odour, hazards (safety), pollution and toxic emission;*

- *Reporting on activities to assist in the preservation and sustainability of resources – choice of transport, ecological impact, reduction and elimination waste and packaging, substitution of raw materials or other inputs, usage of utilities, e.g. gases, water, electricity, new and recycled materials.*

PRIVATE SECTOR

We strive to live our value 'Social Responsibility' by our commitment to corporate social responsibility which is driven by our key strategic themes:

- Learning
- Equality
- Enterprise
- Environment.

These themes have been carefully identified with our community partners and have been recognised by Business in the Community as relevant and critical to the development of society in Northern Ireland.

To ascertain society's perceptions of our community programmes and to assist in the development and review of our community policy and strategy, we have, for the past three years, conducted a survey. Our target audience includes the business sector, community, education, elected representatives and voluntary organisations.

Awareness of our involvement and commitment has increased year on year over the last three years. The extent to which support is given by us 'has met/ exceeded expectations' and has helped raise community profile. The proportion of those who feel that our support 'far exceeded expectations' has doubled in the last year.

In comparison to the companies most approached for community support, this year's survey shows that 79% considered our company to be similar or much better than the benchmark company identified by the research group as the most popular company for sponsorship.

We were awarded the business in the community special award for social responsibility at the 2001 quality awards gala ceremony. This was the first year of the special award, which was presented to recognise outstanding commitment to community investment and social responsibility.

Links to Fundamental Concepts

☐ Leadership and constancy of purpose	☐ Customer focus
	☐ Partner development
☑ Management by process and facts	☑ Public responsibility
☐ People development and involvement	☐ Results orientation
☐ Continuous learning, improvement and innovation	

Criterion 8

PUBLIC SECTOR

Although the school has not conducted a formal survey to establish society's perceptions of the school – not easy when we serve a population of 600,000 – relationships between the school and its neighbourhood are very good and the school is highly regarded by the community in which it is based. Evidence for this can be found in feedback to the Chair of Governors who is also a local councillor, in the high demand for places in the integrated nursery and by comments made by parents of these local nursery children who every year make positive comments on the quality of service provided in the parental survey. Examples from recent Parent Voices include:

- "A brilliant school you run for both children with special needs and local children."
- "Looking at other schools we found our school is highly regarded by other schools."
- "We have never heard anything against the school but lots of good comments even from people that know someone (not direct contact) that's attended."

Most of this has been in the local newspaper but some has reached the nationals. It is worth pointing out that all this has been positive publicity for our youngsters and that we have also had TV coverage – five minutes on BBC North West (7m viewers) and several showings of the Teacher of the Year (three minutes) on the Disney Channel.

SMALL/MEDIUM

We are a small company with an industrial estate on one side and two houses bordered by farmland on the other side.

The company is aware of how it may impact on the local community and takes steps to ensure that it does not impact in any adverse way.

The company is an equal opportunity employer and also follows the fair employment guidelines of the Fair Employment (Northern Ireland) Act 1989.

The company has built strong partnerships with all relevant local authorities. As a consequence of involvement in Investors in People, the Managing Director became a member of the Investors in People recognition panel at the request of the local authority.

The Managing Director keeps in close contact with the local council and has been invited by them to join a steering committee. The steering committee was set up to provide help and advice to local businesses, the Managing Director being asked to act as the small business advisor.

The Managing Director and the Production Manager discussed with one of the neighbouring householders her concerns involving slight nuisance of smoke, smell and dust coming from the factory premises. The smoke and smell had been generated by occasional burning of offcut waste materials. To rectify the problem the offcut waste is now taken offsite and recycled or disposed of by waste specialists.

Links to Fundamental Concepts

- ☐ Leadership and constancy of purpose
- ☑ Management by process and facts
- ☐ People development and involvement
- ☐ Continuous learning, improvement and innovation
- ☐ Customer focus
- ☐ Partner development
- ☑ Public responsibility
- ☐ Results orientation

Links to Fundamental Concepts

- ☐ Leadership and constancy of purpose
- ☑ Management by process and facts
- ☐ People development and involvement
- ☐ Continuous learning, improvement and innovation
- ☐ Customer focus
- ☐ Partner development
- ☑ Public responsibility
- ☐ Results orientation

3.8 | Society Results

What the organisation is achieving in relation to local, national and international society as appropriate.

Sub-criterion 8B:
Performance indicators.

Areas to address may include:

- *Those listed under sub-criterion 8a;*

- *Handling changes in employment levels;*

- *Press coverage;*

- *Dealings with authorities on issues such as – certification, clearances, import/export, planning, product release;*

- *Accolades and awards received.*

PRIVATE SECTOR

A total of 27 measures have been defined covering all aspects of the scope of the society measures. These include a four-year trend showing how the organisation has increased its worldwide community investment from 36 million Euros to over 47 million Euros, a consistent decrease in the level of waste for disposal with the current results being close to target, and an increase in the number and level of investment in water stewardship projects.

The effect of changes on the local community is measured through monitoring the number of jobs transferred during re-structuring programmes. Given the history of a male dominated industry, the number of females in senior positions provides an indication of the effectiveness of the equal opportunities policies. Our top 300 managers are drawn from 33 countries, a growing proportion (21%) are women – up almost 100% since 1992.

In the Philippines we are working in a multi-sector partnership to rehabilitate Manila's polluted river while in China initiatives include planting half a million trees. In Greece our factory recycles its hot water to heat the local school.

Our commitment to sustainability was recognised with our inclusion as an industry group leader in the food products sector of the Dow Jones Sustainability Group Indexes.

In addition to the measures that have improving trends, targets and external comparisons, a number are tracked that indicate society's satisfaction with the organisation. These include positive press coverage and the number of internal environmental award that are given.

Links to Fundamental Concepts

☐ Leadership and constancy of purpose	☐ Customer focus
	☐ Partner development
☑ Management by process and facts	☑ Public responsibility
☐ People development and involvement	☐ Results orientation
☐ Continuous learning, improvement and innovation	

Criterion 8

116

PUBLIC SECTOR

The school contributes to society and the environment in five key ways: its support for charitable and community causes by increasing access to and links with the community to help to break down perceptual barriers between able bodied and handicapped members of society, by its increasing partnership with other mainstream and other special schools (which helps to develop and share good practice in special needs education), by its involvement with local colleges and universities (supporting education and training of students) and finally in its impact on the environment.

Throughout our existence we have supported town and national charities, we have afforded our services and our facilities to a wide range of organisations. These include, in recent years: Macmillan Nurses – World's biggest coffee mornings (annually). Mayor of Oldham's Charity Appeal (annually). Comic Relief (1995, 1997 & 1999). Shelter – Homeless Charity. Down's Syndrome Fashion Show. National Association for Special Educational Needs. Save the Children Fund – money raised by the children running a tuck shop. Sponsored Silence Macmillan Nurse. Poppy Day – Kosovo refugees 12.4.99.

For many years our school nurse, now retired but still active, has co-ordinated and driven lorries with gifts for Romania and now Kosovo, these are well supported by staff and children. This year children sent shoeboxes to Albania and clothes to Kosovo refugees.

In 1991 the Head set up the Coverhill Trust funded from his Health Authority earnings and this makes grants to help individual children or parents, to promote school projects, and other charitable causes which further the ends of the school.

SMALL/MEDIUM

To demonstrate our commitment to the Government's New Deal programme, we have formed a partnership between ourselves, Croxteth Community Trust known as the 580 Partnership and Liverpool Hope University. The scheme is to bring empty homes back into use and has provided a wage and training to 12 individuals under the New Deal for Housing scheme. We are also signed up to the Government programme, by directly employing individuals under the New Deal initiative – so far we have employed two people.

We actively support local Training initiatives, particularly relating to minority groups. We currently have 3 trainees from Merseyside Skills Training on two year training programmes. We have been participating in this scheme for the last ten years and have given permanent employment to most of the trainees who were originally placed with us.

Within our Information Technology section, we have partnered with Blackburn House, Women's Technology and Education Centre and have offered work experience placements so far to 6 women, one of whom is now in permanent employment with us on a part-time basis to enable her to continue studying for a degree in Computer Studies.

We are committed to working with schools within our communities and always react favourably to requests for pupils to gain work experience with us. Locally, The Manufacturing, Science and Finance Trade Union were awarded funding to run their own project – Building trade union capacity to support employee development in the Voluntary sector. One of our members of staff has been trained via this project as a Learning Representative for staff in the Trust and is now working in a partnership arrangement with our Training and Development Manager to improve access to training and development.

Links to Fundamental Concepts

☐ Leadership and constancy of purpose

☑ Management by process and facts

☐ People development and involvement

☐ Continuous learning, improvement and innovation

☐ Customer focus

☐ Partner development

☑ Public responsibility

☐ Results orientation

Links to Fundamental Concepts

☐ Leadership and constancy of purpose

☑ Management by process and facts

☐ People development and involvement

☐ Continuous learning, improvement and innovation

☐ Customer focus

☐ Partner development

☑ Public responsibility

☐ Results orientation

Criterion 8

The Excellence Model

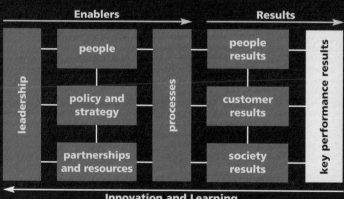

© 1999 EFQM.

"The organisation's achievements, both financial and non-financial, covering results that are planned and operational measures that are used to monitor and predict."

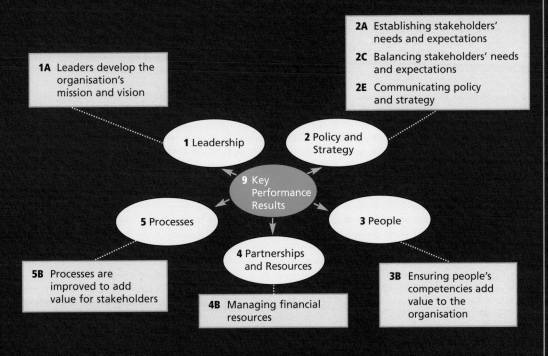

2A Establishing stakeholders' needs and expectations

2C Balancing stakeholders' needs and expectations

2E Communicating policy and strategy

1A Leaders develop the organisation's mission and vision

1 Leadership

2 Policy and Strategy

9 Key Performance Results

5 Processes

4 Partnerships and Resources

3 People

5B Processes are improved to add value for stakeholders

4B Managing financial resources

3B Ensuring people's competencies add value to the organisation

Linkages with the enablers

3.9 | Key Performance Results

What the organisation is achieving in relation to its planned performance.

Sub-criterion 9A:

Key performance outcomes.

Areas to address may include:

- *Financial outcomes including – share price, dividends, gross margins, net profit, sales, meeting of budgets;*

- *Non-financial outcomes including – market share, time to market, volumes, success rates.*

PRIVATE SECTOR

Our success at converting calls to applications has increased year on year, which in book balance terms is an increase of £250 m year on year. We now control 70% of the Career Development Loan market. To improve service, efficiency and reduce costs, Career Development Loans were centralised. The customer now has one central point of contact whereas previously, only 200 out of 2000 offices had Career Development Loan specialists. Our main goal was to migrate the 22,000 existing Career Development Loan accounts within the timescale set, which we were successful in completing. We wrote 8,537 new Career Development Loans totalling £36.4m, against targets of 7,927 and £33.8m respectively.

Profit per loan on file and profit per employee have risen dramatically since 1991. Profit per employee has actually risen by 1563% since 1991.

Fraud can seriously diminish profits and in 1992 we invested in our new fraud detection system which has vast analytical powers and is used to combat fraudulent applications (those customers applying with no intention to repay). We have prevented £42,876,964 worth of fraud since 1991.

Links to Fundamental Concepts

- ☐ Leadership and constancy of purpose
- ☐ Customer focus
- ☐ Partner development
- ☐ Management by process and facts
- ☐ Public responsibility
- ☐ People development and involvement
- ☑ Results orientation
- ☐ Continuous learning, improvement and innovation

Criterion 9

PUBLIC SECTOR We effectively implement an annual maintenance programme for the repair and maintenance of all the Council's property stock which totals 250 schools including Nursery, Primary, Special Educational Need and Secondary education provision.

In each of the past six years we have fully completed the programme within budget. The Authority has been particularly successful in bidding for funding under the Government's New Deal for Schools Initiative and has delivered impressive capital programme projects such as the development of Rugby Library, the Leamington Pump Rooms Library, Camp Hill Family and Community Care Centre and the £25m Schools Reorganisation Programme.

We were able to respond to a very tight timescale and deliver the first three phases on time and within budget. Lease terms have been agreed to specifically allow flexibility for the new tenants, which has resulted in increased occupancy and thus improved job creation opportunities.

As part of the County's philosophy to develop identifiable trading areas we have extended trading accounts. These now extend to cover the urban and rural estates areas.

Over the last six years an under spend of £677,000 was achieved in the business unit functions.

We have developed a new computerised Rent Management System to enable the department to take responsibility for the collection of rent for the whole of the County Council. Previously individual departments had undertaken this. As a result of these changes we identified additional rents of £20,000 and also identified an overpayment of VAT of £27,000 that was subsequently recovered.

SMALL/MEDIUM The reporting of business results is strong. Fiscal reporting is very formalised, budgets are produced and updated with forecasts.

When the company is compared to others in the United Kingdom Benchmark Index survey, its Business, or Key Performance, Results have been in the top 10% for the last 4 years and the top 3% for the last 3 years. This performance is the more creditable when one considers that we are being compared to companies in the successful electronics sector.

Three key areas of performance for us are Gross Profit Margin, Break-even analysis and Turnover. The gross profit margin performance is excellent compared to the UK small company average, which is quoted at 50%. Turnover per employee has risen in the last 4 years with a 20 % rise in the last year. Gross profit per employee has risen over the last 5 years, which is a gain of over 50% during this time period and a 10% rise on last year. Net profit per employee has risen over the last 4 years and significantly over the last 12 months with a 62% rise.

Another area that has produced good results is in the reduction of debtor days. We have seen a year on year reduction for the last 4 years.

Links to Fundamental Concepts

- ☐ Leadership and constancy of purpose
- ☐ Management by process and facts
- ☐ People development and involvement
- ☐ Continuous learning, improvement and innovation
- ☐ Customer focus
- ☐ Partner development
- ☐ Public responsibility
- ☑ Results orientation

Links to Fundamental Concepts

- ☐ Leadership and constancy of purpose
- ☐ Management by process and facts
- ☐ People development and involvement
- ☐ Continuous learning, improvement and innovation
- ☐ Customer focus
- ☐ Partner development
- ☐ Public responsibility
- ☑ Results orientation

Criterion 9

3.9 | Key Performance Results

What the organisation is achieving in relation to its planned performance.

Sub-criterion 9B:

Key performance indicators.

Areas to address may include:

- *Processes – performance, deployment, assessments, innovations, improvements, cycle times, defect rate, maturity, productivity, time to market;*

- *External resources including partnerships – supplier performance, supplier price, number and value added of partnerships, number and value added of innovative products and services solutions generated by partners, number and value added of joint improvements with partners, recognition of partners' contribution;*

- *Financial – cash flow items, balance sheet items, depreciation, maintenance costs, return on equity, return on net assets, credit ratings;*

- *Buildings, equipment and materials – defect rates, inventory turnover, utility consumption, utilisation;*

- *Technology – innovation rate, value of intellectual property, patents, royalties;*

- *Information and knowledge – accessibility, integrity, relevance, timeliness, sharing and using knowledge, value of intellectual capital.*

PRIVATE SECTOR

The business uses a series of key indicators to predict what is happening to the outcomes. In this way we are able to adapt processes and change strategies to address issues before they have significant impact on the outcomes. The main indicators are:

Occupancy – a key indicator of yield premium given as a percentage of room availability.

Rooms sold – the absolute number of rooms sold provides a clear indication of success and a key indicator of total revenue. Up 17% last year.

Average rates – this represents the average rate earned per occupied room and is a further indicator of yield premium, measured in £s up 5%.

We also consider the performance of each element of the service we provide to be an indicator of our overall performance outcomes. For example, we consider the food and beverage revenue we generate for each of our occupied rooms. Information on revenue on food and beverage is tracked monthly. This enables us to predict potential problems and make necessary adjustments. To ensure this increase in revenue is adding value to the business and is not simply achieved through discounting we also track the food and liquor margins as a percentage of the turnover. Conference revenue is also tracked monthly to help predict problems with total revenue. This has risen by nearly 20% this year. With the growth in leisure time we have recognised the need to focus attention on the growth of our golf and leisure elements of the business. In addition to tracking the revenue we gain from these business we also track the growth in the business by focusing on the membership numbers. This area has seen a 20% growth in revenue year on year.

Links to Fundamental Concepts

- ☐ Leadership and constancy of purpose
- ☐ Management by process and facts
- ☐ People development and involvement
- ☐ Continuous learning, improvement and innovation
- ☐ Customer focus
- ☐ Partner development
- ☐ Public responsibility
- ☑ Results orientation

Our key additional measures of the organisation's performance results are driven by enabler action from Leadership, Policy and Strategy, and Processes.

Our quality projects database contains more than 350 projects, including research, audit, and opinion surveys. We also submit all our research projects to the National Research Register. Examples of such projects include:

Psychological therapies – the impact of confrontation of abusers by survivors of childhood sexual abuse.

Psychological Therapies Outcome Study. This has benefited clients/commissioners by
- helping clients to comment on their needs before being seen
- getting feedback from clients on outcome and quality of service
- feeding back outcome measures to clinicians
- improving service audit and ability to feed back info to GPs, commissioners, and the Trust.

Analysis of Repertory Grid data in Clinical Psychology Process Research.

Child and Adolescent Psychiatry – Use of the Hospital Anxiety Depression scale with adolescents. The standardisation of the Hospital Anxiety and Depression scale for use with adolescents project has led to changes in outcome measures, so that clients in child psychiatry are now monitored more regularly than they were.

Although most of the required training is identified from the annual Training Needs Analysis, training programmes are also arranged to respond to new demand in-year. For example, the number of training sessions offered by the Training and Development Unit for last year was initially 245. A number of sessions were added throughout the year, (e.g. approximately 100 Handling and Moving sessions, 28 Health a Safety sessions, and a further 50 Information Management and Technology training sessions) giving a total of 423 sessions.

The company has published results for the past five years producing Company Report which was circulated in the company and thus to all stakeholders.

Competitors are not required to publish detailed data under exemptions for small businesses and the larger competitors' results are consolidated into group accounts. Estimates of competitor performance have been produced using the limited published data, credit reports and information from trade contacts.

Assumptions have been made, using our performance levels on ratios such as Debtors and Creditors, and the results indicate that the company is performing significantly better in profitability terms. Turning to more detailed, secondary financial measures, the United Kingdom Benchmark Index has many lower level financial performance ratios, although true comparison is always problematic owing to different reporting methodologies. With so many measures it is impossible for the company to excel in all the areas, indeed some are adversely affected by improvements in others. Of the 11 key performance indicators, 8 show an upward trend and 3 are about even. On the Business Excellence Benchmark, 6 indicators show an upward trend, 3 are stable.

The Board of Directors has reviewed this performance and is generally satisfied, but has used the figures to generate more specific policies in some areas. An example is Debtor Days, with such a high level of export sales; we are probably performing better than indicated, but as a safeguard Debtor Insurance has been taken out. The company is using the external benchmark as a measure to drive down debtor days, by focusing on the performance levels of our peers, even though we expect that their performance is mainly UK related. Terms given for most export orders are 60 days, and exports account for 90+% of turnover.

Links to Fundamental Concepts

- ☐ Leadership and constancy of purpose
- ☐ Customer focus
- ☐ Management by process and facts
- ☐ Partner development
- ☐ Public responsibility
- ☐ People development and involvement
- ☑ Results orientation
- ☐ Continuous learning, improvement and innovation

Links to Fundamental Concepts

- ☐ Leadership and constancy of purpose
- ☐ Customer focus
- ☐ Management by process and facts
- ☐ Partner development
- ☐ Public responsibility
- ☐ People development and involvement
- ☑ Results orientation
- ☐ Continuous learning, improvement and innovation

Criterion 9

Appendix A1

 PRIVATE SECTOR **Private Sector Companies**

3663
Leading food-service provider in the catering industry operating a nationwide network of distribution depots and employing over 4,000 personnel.

Agilent Technology (formerly Hewlett Packard)
A division of Hewlett Packard concerned with the design, manufacture and supply of electronic medical equipment.

Barclays Direct Loan Service
Part of the Barclays Group, employing 644 people and providing phone-a-loan and postal loan service to both Barclays and non-Barclays customers.

BAE Systems
Formerly British Aerospace Military Aircraft and Aerostructures, employing over 18,000 people. Designs, develops, manufactures and supports military aircraft, aircraft structures and associated systems.

Bradford and Bingley Plc.
The central support area for savings and customer contact is the result of the Bradford and Bingley Building Society converting to plc status in December 2000. Has a direct savings unit as well as facilitating frontline sales. The area is also responsible for manufacturing all BBGS savings products.

BT Business Advance
Business Advance is an organisation of 2,000 people within BT Retail, which employs 50,000 people. It is responsible for the provision and repair of large networks for customers.

BT Payphones
With a total of 2,038 employees, its business areas are public street payphones, service payphones on privately owned sites and supplying and renting payphones.

Compass Group
The largest food-service organisation in the UK and Ireland, Compass provides high quality catering and support services at over 8,400 locations, serving nearly 3 million meals per day – in staff restaurants, student refectories, hospitals (patient meals), schools, coffee shops, military bases, and via executive dining and corporate hospitality.

DHL International (UK) Limited
Providing express, door-to-door distribution world-wide, including the overnight delivery of light to medium weight freight and documentation within Europe; employing over 3,500 staff.

Marriott Hotels
Marriott Hotels UK, a part of the Whitbread Hotel Company, offers two main types of property: Marriott Hotels – upscale hotels and country clubs; Courtyard Hotels – mid-range hotels situated close to major travel routes.

NatWest Insurance Services
A wholly owned subsidiary of National Westminster Bank plc, employing 1,315 staff, and providing general insurance and independent financial advice.

NatWest Mortgage Services
Provides residential mortgage finance and employs 1,600 staff.

Nortel
A division of the Canadian company Northern Telecom Limited. Nortel employs 900 people and supplies networked communications solutions to telecommunications service providers.

Northern Ireland Electricity
A private sector organisation dedicated to providing a reliable and cost effective service to customers. The core business is made up of Power Procurement Business, NIE Energy Business, Transmission & Distribution Business and Powerteam.

NSK Bearings
NSK Bearings is a manufacturing operation employing 730 people manufacturing rolling ball bearings for the automotive and industrial markets in Europe.

Post Office Counters
Employs 12,300 staff. Services include benefit payment, corporate banking, personal banking, savings, insurance, bill payment, bureau de change, mails, telecommunications, lotteries and stationery.

Rolls Royce
A operational unit within the airline business of Rolls Royce, employing 2300 people in the building and testing of both experimental and production of aero engines.

Siemens Communications Ltd.
A company employing approximately 2500 people operating in the UK public communications market, its activities include design, development, marketing, sales, consultancy, distribution, installation, maintenance and network management.

Unilever HPC-E
The European division of Unilever which develops, manufactures and markets products for home and personal care. Brands include Persil, Sure, Lynx, Jif, Organics and Comfort.

Yell Ltd.
A privately owned company employing over 3,000 people providing classified business information in the form of printed directories and electronic media to business and residential customers.

> The organisation names in Appendix A1 represent a cumulative list of participants in both *The Model in Practice* and *The Model in Practice 2*. All names were correct at the time of original publication.

Appendix A1 (continued)

 Public Sector Organisations

The Bawburgh School
Primary school catering for pupils aged from 4 to 11. 110 pupils are currently on roll.

Civil Service College
As the largest management school in the country, provides training and development to managers and specialists in government.

Central Office of Communication Publications Group
An executive agency commissioning print and publishing services, and producing a wide range of publications – annual reports, periodicals, White Papers, leaflets, posters and web sites.

Circle 33 Housing Group
One of the largest Registered Social Landlords (RSLs) in the UK providing over 20,000 homes to people in need in London and East Anglia.

Devon Social Services
Part of Devon County Council with responsibility for the welfare of the people in Devon, and working with other organisations to provide a range of both counselling and practical services to meet individual needs.

DERA
Part of the Ministry of Defence responsible for technological developments.

DSS IT Services Agency
Provides information systems and information technology services to support social security provision.

Employment Services South West
Agency within the Department for Education and Employment helping people to find work and employers to fill vacancies. One of nine regions making up the national Employment Service in Britain.

Foxdenton School and Integrated Nursery
State primary school for children aged 2–11 catering primarily for those with special educational needs arising from physical or medical difficulties.

Gloucester District Land Registry
The Land Registry is a Government Agency, responsible to the Lord Chancellor, for the delivery of land registration services to England and Wales. The Agency has expanded rapidly with the growth of property activity and is a large regional organisation now comprising 24 District Land Registries with administrative headquarters in central London.

HM Customs and Excise, London Central Collection
Collection of VAT from employers and traders in the London region.

Humberside Police E Division
Protects, helps and re-assures the people of Humberside. Reduces crime and the fear of crime in partnership with other agencies.

Inland Revenue Accounts Office, Cumbernauld
Has responsibility for tax collection, banking and accounting of tax and national insurance contributions.

Inland Revenue Accounts Office, Shipley
Public sector organisation, part of the Inland Revenue. Its main roles are to bank and account for tax and national insurance contributions and to keep accurate and up-to-date records for customers in Southern England, Wales and Northern Ireland. There are 100 people in Shipley.

Inland Revenue NICO Insolvency Group
An executive agency within the DSS with responsibility for national insurance contributions.

Maritime and Coastguard Agency
A government executive agency for maritime safety and search and rescue throughout the UK coastline and waters carrying out inspections of UK registered vessels and vessels visiting the UK ports. The Agency provides a 24-hour emergency co-ordination response from a network of 18 co-ordinated rescues around the UK and employs 1100 staff and 3100 volunteer coastguards.

Northumberland County Council, Operational Services
Operational Services is the delivery arm of Northumberland County Council. Its Contract and Highways Design departments provide a wide range of services and support.

Runshaw College
A tertiary college providing both A levels and vocational course to adults and school leavers, serving over 20,000 students.

Scottish Homes
A national housing agency enabling the effective provision of good quality housing and to stimulate self-motivated communities.

South Yorkshire Police
Policing of South Yorkshire.

Valuation Office Agency
The Valuation Office Agency is an executive agency of the Inland Revenue. Its purpose is to undertake valuations of land and buildings in England, Wales and Scotland in return for fees from public sector clients. It has a business turnover of £165m per annum and provides valuations for business rates and council tax purposes as well as other valuation services.

Warwickshire County Council – Property Services Department
The Property Services Department of the Warwickshire County Council is the department with responsibility as 'landlord' for the effective management of the Council's land and property assets.

Appendix A2

SMEs and Divisional Units

Aeroquip Aerospace Division
Employs around 80 people in designing, manufacturing and supplying fluid handling products to UK aerospace original equipment manufacturers.

AP Acrefair
Air Products' European manufacturing facility employing around 285 people and manufacturing key items of cryogenic plant.

City Technology College
College for over 1,300 pupils serving East Birmingham and North Solihull.

Ducker Engineering
Small business manufacturing, installing and servicing equipment for the garment sector of the industrial laundry market, producing on-hanger finishing, sorting, folding and transportation systems for the workwear rental sector.

Lawson Mardon Plastics
Employs around 150 people in designing and manufacturing injection moulded packaging for the food, beverage, cosmetics and healthcare industries.

Liverpool Housing Trust
The Trust is a Registered Social Landlord working in Merseyside and Cheshire.

Mason Communications Ltd.
Leading European independent telecommunications and IT consultancy delivering business solutions to private and public organisations worldwide. Mason combines business understanding with technical expertise to help clients de-risk the journey.

Police Rehabilitation and Training Trust
The trust has assisted more than 1500 former and serving police officers of the Royal Ulster Constabulary and the Royal Ulster Constabulary Full Time Reserve with rehabilitation, retraining, psychological and physiotherapy services.

Power Innovations Ltd.
A privately owned company employing 170 people manufacturing a large range of semi-conductor overvoltage components for the telecomms protection market.

Scottish Courage Brands
Markets and distributes beer and lager brands in the UK and cross-Channel take-home markets.

Seaview Hotel and Restaurant
An independent owner-managed, small seaside hotel comprising 16 bedrooms, 2 restaurants and 2 bars, with a workforce of 40, serving both the year-round local and tourist trade.

Springfarm Architectural Mouldings
A privately owned company manufacturing a range of architectural mouldings which are sold through builders merchants to the construction and DIY industries.

Vista Optics Limited
A privately owned company with 17 employees, manufacturing medical device polymers for intra-ocular and contact lenses.

References

L.J. Porter and S.J. Tanner, *Assessing Business Excellence*, Butterworth-Heinemann,1998.

Hendricks, K. B., and Singhal, V. R., "Does Implementing an Effective TQM Program Actually Improve Operating Performance: Empirical Evidence From Firms that Have Won Quality Awards", *Management Science*, Vol. 44, No. 9, pp. 1258–1274, 1997.

Hendricks, K. B., and Singhal, V. R., "Don't Count TQM Out", *Quality Progress*, April 1999, pp. 35–42; reprinted in *The Quality Yearbook*, 2000 edn., James W. Cortada and John A. Woods (eds.), McGraw-Hill.

Various award-winning documents (available from the BQF).

Noriaki Kano et al., *Quality*, Union of Japanese Scientists and Engineers, Tokyo, April 1983.

John Bicheno, *The Quality 60, A Guide for Service and Manufacturing*, PICSIE Books, 1998.

Available from the British Quality Foundation

- *How to use the Model*
- *Manage your processes ... using the Excellence Model*
- *Listen to your employees and involve them in improvement ... using the Excellence Model*
- *Manage your organisation ... using the Excellence Model*
- *Drive continuous improvement ... using the Excellence Model*
- *Find out how good you really are ... using the Excellence Model*
- *BQFsnapshot* (self evaluation against the fundamental concepts of excellence software tool)
- *Excellence One* (online learning platform), (EFQM)
- *The EFQM Excellence Model: Companies Version*
- *The EFQM Excellence Model: Public and Voluntary Sector*
- *The Eight Essentials of Excellence*
- *Assessing for Excellence*

Glossary of Terms to Help with Use and Understanding of the EFQM Excellence Model

Creativity
The generation of ideas for new or improved working practices and/or products and services.

Culture
The total range of behaviours, ethics and values that are transmitted, practised and reinforced by members of the organisation.

Enablers
Enabler criteria are concerned with how the organisation approaches each of the activities suggested by the criterion parts.

Ethics
The universal morals that the organisation adopts and abides by.

Excellence
Outstanding practice in managing the organisation and achieving results based on fundamental concepts.

External Customers
The end customers of the organisation. These may also include other customers in the distribution chain (see also internal customers).

Finances
The short-term funds required for the day-to-day operation, and the capital funding required for the longer term financing, of the organisation.

Innovation
The practical translation of ideas into new products, services, processes, systems and social interactions.

Internal Customers
The recipients of the outputs of processes within an organisation.

Knowledge
Part of the hierarchy of data, information and knowledge. Data is raw facts; information is data with context and perspective; knowledge is information with guidance for action.

Leaders
The people who co-ordinate and balance the interests of all who have a stake in the organisation, including the executive team, all other managers and those in team leadership positions or with a subject leadership role.

Learning
The acquiring and understanding of information which may lead to improvement or change. Organisational learning activities include benchmarking, assessments, audits and best practice studies. Individual learning activities include training and professional qualifications.

Management System
The framework of processes and procedures used to ensure that the organisation can fulfil all tasks required to achieve its objectives.

Mission
A statement that describes the purpose of an organisation – why it exists.

Partnerships
A working relationship between two or more parties creating added value for the customer. Partners can include suppliers, distributors, joint ventures and alliances.

People
All of the individuals employed by the organisation, including full-time, part-time, contract and temporary employees.

Perception
The opinion of an individual or group of people.

Performance
A measure of attainment achieved by an individual, team, organisation or process.

Process
A sequence of activities that adds value by producing required outputs from a variety of inputs.

RADAR
Results, Approach, Deployment, Assessment and Review.

Results
Result criteria are concerned with what the organisation has achieved or is achieving.

Stakeholders
All those who have an interest in an organisation, its activities and achievements. These may include customers, partners, employees, shareholders, owners, government and regulators.

Society
All those who are, or believe they are, affected by an organisation, other than its people, customers and partners.

Values
The understandings and expectations that describe how the organisation's people behave and upon which all business relationships are based, e.g. trust, support and truth.

Vision
A statement that describes how the organisation wishes to be in the future.